LEADING WOMEN

Actress and Activist

Kerry Washington

JOEL NEWSOME

Cavendish
Square

New York

Published in 2018 by Cavendish Square Publishing, LLC
243 5th Avenue, Suite 136, New York, NY 10016

Library of Congress Cataloging-in-Publication Data

Names: Newsome, Joel author.
Title: Kerry Washington : actress and activist / Joel Newsome.
Description: New York : Cavendish Square Publishing, 2018. | Series: Leading women | Includes
bibliographical references and index.
Identifiers: LCCN 2017015467 (print) | LCCN 2017028882 (ebook) | ISBN
9781502631756 (E-book) | ISBN 9781502631749 (library bound) | ISBN 9781502634139 (pbk.)
Subjects: LCSH: Washington, Kerry, 1977- | Actors--United States--Biography.
| African American women political activists--Biography.
Classification: LCC PN2287.W4524 (ebook) | LCC PN2287.W4524 N49 2017 (print) | DDC
791.4302/8092 [B] --dc23
LC record available at https://lccn.loc.gov/2017015467

Editorial Director: David McNamara
Editor: Jodyanne Benson
Copy Editor: Nathan Heidelberger
Associate Art Director: Amy Greenan
Designer: Renni Johnson
Production Coordinator: Karol Szymczuk
Photo Research: J8 Media

CONTENTS

CHAPTER ONE

Introducing Kerry Washington

Whether she is portraying Ray Charles's wife, a brilliant Washington crisis manager, or Anita Hill during her tense testimony in front of the United States Senate Judiciary Committee, Kerry Washington connects with audiences by conveying a complex interplay between **vulnerability** and strength. Her upbringing, set in the culturally diverse Bronx within a socially aware, educated black family, has had much to do with the way she approaches both her acting roles

Kerry Washington (*front row, center*) poses with her eighth-grade chorus group at the Spence School in 1990.

and her engagement with social justice issues. While many successful actors have causes that are important to them, Kerry Washington has actively supported a variety of campaigns and institutions geared toward making our world a more equal and inclusive place. A vocal **advocate** for actors of color, she has spoken out about how Hollywood tends to typecast actors of color and the importance of being involved in not just the performance but the creative process of making films. With credits for producing to her name, Kerry Washington is striving to be an example not just for actors of color but for those interested in creating a more just world. From her work with the Obama administration to her collaboration with the skincare company Neutrogena, Washington has used her celebrity to create change and draw attention to issues that have been important to her from a very young age. In fact, Washington's upbringing was centered on the value of being an informed and engaged citizen.

A Girl from the Bronx

Kerry Marisa Washington was born on January 31, 1977. She was raised in the Bronx, New York City, by her parents, Earl Washington, who is a real estate agent, and Valerie Washington, a professor of early elementary education at Lehman College. Her parents were very politically conscious and sought to expose Kerry to the world of ideas early in life. At thirteen, Kerry attended an event at Yankee Stadium to see the newly freed anti-apartheid activist Nelson Mandela speak. The value of being socially informed was highlighted throughout her upbringing. In a 2013 interview with *Vanity Fair*, Washington said, "My becoming a voting citizen was celebrated the way other people would celebrate a Sweet 16. My parents took me out to dinner, and we talked about who I was going to vote for."[1]

While both of Kerry Washington's parents encouraged her to be socially aware and form her own opinions, differing points of view sometimes divided the Washington household. Clarence Thomas was nominated to the Supreme Court in 1991, and his vetting was scandalized by allegations of sexual harassment made by Anita Hill, a law professor who had previously been a subordinate to Thomas. Though Kerry was only fourteen at the time of the hearings, she remembers being aware of the complicated identity conflicts that characterized the family debate regarding Anita Hill's testimony.

My understanding was mostly shaped, at the time, by my parents. They were both really struggling, because usually in my house everybody was on the same page with ideology, whether it was a woman's right to choose or affirmative action. But this was one of those moments where my parents had a different opinion about what might be happening. My dad, as an African-American man, had a certain sense of understanding of the dynamics of racial discrimination. My mom, as a woman, while she understood the dynamics of racial discrimination, was

> *also engaging with what was unfolding as a woman, from a perspective of gender. It was one of the first moments where I kind of realized that my understanding of myself, when I fold in race and gender, may be more complex than I knew it to be at the time.*[2]

This complex understanding of the interplay of her identities must have fueled Washington's portrayal of Anita Hill in the HBO film *Confirmation*, which depicts Hill's testimony during the Clarence Thomas hearings. Kerry Washington was deeply involved in the project as the lead actor, and she also gave her talents as an executive producer of the film.

The Desire to Perform

The Washingtons were not directly connected to the entertainment industry during Kerry's childhood. However, some of her acquaintances would also enjoy celebrity status as adults. Washington attended the elite Spence School, a private all-girls academy on Manhattan's Upper East Side. Gwyneth Paltrow was one of her classmates, and the two sang together in an a cappella singing troupe while Washington was a junior and Paltrow was a senior. As a child, Washington spent time at the Kips Bay Boys and Girls Club in the Bronx, where she took dance lessons from Larry Maldonado, who founded and ran the club's performing arts program. When Maldonado was busy with other

Washington spent time developing her childhood interests at the Kips Bay Boys and Girls Club in New York City.

tasks, Washington's dance class learned from a talented substitute who would eventually leave New York for Los Angeles to pursue a dance career. Washington credits that substitute, Jennifer Lopez, for teaching her all her best moves.

In addition to dance and singing, Washington was involved in a variety of extracurricular activities throughout her childhood. In a 2010 interview, Washington explained, "I had two parents who worked full time and rather than just be a latchkey kid, I did

The Spence School

The Spence School, which Washington attended along with Gwyneth Paltrow, is an all-girls independent school in New York City. It was founded in 1892 by Clara B. Spence. As a civil and women's rights advocate who lived openly with another woman and adopted four children, Spence was a woman ahead of her time. She was passionate about providing equal educational opportunities for women and worked to expose her students to major thinkers. Helen Keller, Edith Wharton, and Booker T. Washington all spoke at the school while Clara was running it. This dedication to well-rounded intellect is reflected in the school's motto, *non scholae sed vitae discimus*, which means "Not for school but for life we learn."

This storied history of educational activism must have appealed to the Washingtons as they moved Kerry from public school to Spence after her sixth-grade year. In addition to the theater and singing opportunities, Washington was exposed to a rigorous and diverse liberal arts and sciences and foreign language curriculum. The English coursework includes classes in African American, Asian, African, Caribbean, Latin American and Middle Eastern literature. Clara B. Spence said her institution was "a place not of mechanical instruction but a school of character where the common requisites for all have been human feeling, a sense of humor, and the spirit of intellectual and moral adventure."[3] Washington would carry her humor, intellect, and adventure from Spence to George Washington University.

Washington spent her high school years at the historic Spence School.

activities: Monday was ballet, Tuesday was gymnastics, Wednesday was the children's theater company, Thursday was piano."[4] She was inspired to take up swimming partly because her parents pointed out that expertise in the sport might someday save someone's life. Washington's interest in swimming dovetailed with her earliest career ambition. "I wanted to work with Shamu at Sea World," Washington confessed. "I thought that was the best job in the world, to care for and feed dancing whales."[5]

While Washington would not go on to pursue a career caring for marine life, she continued to structure her life around endeavors that aligned with her values as she grew older. As a teenager, she got a chance to fuse her love of acting with social activism when she became a safe-sex advocate in Mount Sinai's Adolescent Health Center. Washington and other young actors participated in an educational ensemble that performed original sex education sketches in local community centers and learning institutions. These sketches demanded raw emotional connection with the characters that the young actors portrayed. In one sketch, Washington was cast as the sister of a young man wrestling with the fact that their father is gay and recently tested positive for HIV. She credits the experience of using theater as a means of education for preparing her for her future in emotionally resonant dramatic roles. "It was some of the best actor training I've ever had. We would stay in character after the show, and the audience would interact with us. It taught me the importance of really understanding everything about who you're playing, because you never knew what question was going to come."[6] Washington must have reflected upon these early sketches while preparing for her first major motion picture, *Save the Last Dance*, in which she plays a teenage mother who assists the main character (portrayed by Julia Stiles) in navigating an interracial relationship and adjusting to her new Chicago neighborhood.

As a native New Yorker, Washington was an avid theatergoer as a child and enjoyed Broadway shows as often as possible. She explained in an interview, "It was the way that we celebrated different rites of passage—like my graduation from sixth grade was seeing *Into the Woods*. Birthdays, anniversaries, holidays, good report cards—those things were celebrated with trips to the theater."[7] Washington had a flair for the dramatic even then. Growing up, Washington's grandmother used to call her "Sarah" in reference to the French actress Sarah Bernhardt, who gained worldwide fame on the stage and later appeared in silent films when the medium emerged. Eventually, Washington would make her own mark on the New York stage when she made her Broadway debut playing Susan, the only female character, in David Mamet's play *Race*.

While Washington has made a point not to talk too much about her private life in interviews, she has talked openly about race and gender and discussed how these identities inform her work as a performer. Though some actors might eschew these subjects in favor of less controversial topics, Washington has shared nuanced insight on how being a woman of color has impacted her experience in Hollywood, in terms of the roles she has been considered for and how she engages with the characters she depicts. In a 2013 interview with the *Guardian*, Washington explained the complex nature of the influence her race has had on her career:

There are two sides to this coin. I have had, and still do, experiences where someone will say, "You know, we just don't really see this character as black. We don't want to go black with her." Some of it I respect, because this is a visual medium, so I don't believe in color-blind casting. But I think sometimes people make that decision out of fear, or laziness, or just not wanting to have to travel down roads that aren't familiar.[8]

One positive experience for Washington, as an actress of color, was being cast as the lead in Shonda Rhimes's political drama *Scandal*, which centers around Olivia Pope, a Washington, DC, fixer who assists high-powered politicians and elites with managing public-image crises. Pope's character is based on real-life crisis manager Judy Smith, who worked for President George W. Bush and is an African American woman.

Struggling with Image

As a child, Washington struggled to see herself as pretty, partly because she felt self-conscious about her skin tone. In an interview with Oprah Winfrey, Washington explained, "Another young woman I grew up with was much fairer skinned than I was, with much straighter hair, and that meant that she was prettier."[9] As a means of compensating for her appearance, Washington focused on developing her intellect, sense of humor, and other personality traits. Though she was motivated by a sense of not being pretty enough, the choice to foster her inner qualities helped Washington to realize the value of her unique personality. While examining her reluctance

Washington struggled with her image as a young person but has become a champion for inclusivity in the beauty industry.

to mold herself based on the desires of Hollywood, Washington stated, "Most of the beginning of my life I was fighting the idea that I was not enough. That I had to be fixed … I think I spent the first twenty years of my life trying to be somebody else, so I just don't have the energy at this point."[10]

At this point in her career, fans are following Washington for the simple fact that she does not compromise herself in pursuit of success. She has become a spokesperson for both L'Oréal and Neutrogena, the latter of which also named her creative consultant as she helped the brand develop fourteen new shades of makeup for people with darker skin tones in an effort to make beauty products more inclusive.

A Bright Future

While Washington was a self-described dramatic child who was interested in performance at a young age, she didn't grow up wanting to make a life in the arts. An intense advanced placement (AP) biology course in high school brought on her realization that a career as a marine biologist (and someday swimming at Sea World with Shamu) was not for her. Though she was active in drama productions at Spence and joined the Screen Actors Guild as a teen, acting was not where she saw herself professionally.

She considered various paths in **psychology** as well as following in her mother's footsteps with a career in education, but while in college, she slowly made her way toward a commitment to making a living through performance. Though she was accepted to such prestigious theater conservatories as the Tisch School of the Arts at New York University and Carnegie Mellon School of Drama, Washington chose to attend George

Washington University, in part because her scholarship there did not require her to study theater exclusively. During her undergraduate years, Washington focused her studies on psychology and **anthropology** as well as acting. This well-rounded approach to her education continues to influence the way Washington understands the characters she portrays.

She would spend her years at George Washington University being mentored by theater professionals before applying her curious intellectual lens to the portrayal of characters in the theater department of George Washington University and beyond. Washington grew up a socially conscious performer valuing the life of the mind. What makes Washington unique as an actress is how she would eventually bring her education and interest in activism to her roles. Her intelligence and activism have led her to become a strong role model for men and women everywhere.

"One of the best films
I've seen this year.
Revolutionary."
A.O. Scott, The New York Times

OUR SONG

lift every voice.

The highly-acclaimed new film from the director of GIRLS TOWN.

INDEPENDENT FILM CHANNEL PRODUCTIONS PRESENTS IN ASSOCIATION WITH JOURNEYMAN PICTURES AND BEECH HILL FILMS A C-HUNDRED FILM CORP. MOVIE "OUR SONG"

ANNA SIMPSON KERRY WASHINGTON AND THE JACKIE ROBINSON STEPPERS MARCHING BAND CASTING DIRECTOR ALEXA L. FOGEL DIRECTOR OF PHOTOGRAPHY JIM DENAULT

JULIE PANEBIANCO CO-PRODUCERS ALEXA L. FOGEL JOSEPH INFANTOLINO EXECUTIVE PRODUCERS CAROLINE KAPLAN JONATHAN SEHRING MICHAEL

PRODUCED BY JIM McKAY PAUL MEZEY DIANA E. WILLIAMS WRITTEN AND DIRECTED BY JIM McKAY

IFC Films

oursong.net

CHAPTER TWO

Early Successes

After performing in productions at Spence and performing in educational theater at schools and hospitals, Washington took her acting talents to college at George Washington University. Though acting had given Washington great creative satisfaction, she did not choose to major in drama. Instead, Washington created her own course of study at George Washington, which allowed her to double major in anthropology and **sociology**. While Washington was looking at human development and interaction in the classroom, she was required to audition for each production that George Washington put on. Kerry Washington was able to develop both her intellect and

A promotional poster for Washington's first motion picture, *Our Song* her creative talents in college, and she would soon learn how to bring both to her work on-screen.

A College Mentor

In 2006, Denzel Washington's inspirational book *A Hand to Guide Me* featured the voices of more than seventy modern legends in sports, business, the arts, and politics telling stories about the power of receiving mentorship. Kerry Washington was included in the project, and she explained how Stacy Wolf, a professor at George Washington University, taught her how to bring her intellectual interests into alignment with her creative pursuits.

I'd always felt there was a disconnect between being intellectual and creative—that you had to be one or the other. But at school I met this wonderful professor named Stacy Wolf. She was the first person I knew who represented the amalgamation of both. She was a professor in the theater and dance department, but she taught performance studies and theater history. She put the thing that I had loved the most into an intellectual framework.

I had an incredible experience in tenth grade playing Ophelia at the same time we were studying Hamlet in English class. It was serendipitous and the first time I was able to apply what I was learning in the classroom to what I was doing onstage. It was brief but exhilarating, and I wondered if it would ever happen for me again. And then I met Stacy, whose whole life was all about theater as more than just the imagination.

Washington's alma mater, The George Washington University

> *Imagination is fundamental to what I do, but one of the things I love most about acting is placing it in the context of the history and sociology and psychology and politics of a certain time or place. I really learned how to do that with Stacy.*[1]

With Stacy Wolf's guidance, Washington worked hard to find the voice of each character she portrayed at George Washington University. She took advantage of the opportunity in school to bring her heart to the theater and her mind to the classroom. After college, she spent some time in India learning yoga and Indian theater before coming back to the United States to try to make a living as a professional actress.

Getting Started

After graduating, Washington began to pursue professional acting while also working as a substitute teacher. In 2000, she performed the role of Lanisha Brown in the independent film *Our Song*. The movie details the lives of three Brooklyn teenagers who are in the Jackie Robinson Steppers Marching Band. The young women find themselves at a crossroads when they learn over summer vacation that their high school won't reopen and they will have to find new schools to attend. The film explores teen pregnancy and gun violence. Roger Ebert gave the film three stars, praised its patience in detailing teenage angst and uncertainty, and said that Washington "has a face the camera loves."[2]

A year later, *Save the Last Dance* appeared in theaters featuring Washington's first role in a major motion picture. Washington plays Chenille, a teen mother who befriends Sara, played by Julia Stiles, a white girl who recently moved to a gritty Chicago neighborhood. Chenille is friendly but not two-dimensional. When Sara starts dating Chenille's brother, Derek, Chenille challenges Sara by explaining how hard it is for black women to see Sara with an ambitious, educated black man like Derek. In a 2014 interview with *Allure* magazine, Washington looked back on her portrayal of Chenille and how she had strived "to make sure the character wasn't a stereotype, but that she felt like a real person … Especially for me, as a woman and as a person

Julia Stiles (*left*) and Kerry Washington (*right*) are shown in a still from the major motion picture *Save the Last Dance*.

of color, I play these roles where many people in society may never think about that person. I knew that there were going to be special challenges to being a woman of color as an actor."[3]

Save the Last Dance was the number-one movie in North America two weekends in a row and brought in $131 million as well as a number of **accolades** from the MTV Movie Awards and Teen Choice Awards. Washington's star was beginning to rise. She continued to substitute teach, though some changes needed to be made. Due to the popularity of *Save the Last Dance* among some of her older students, she started to be recognized for her work in movies. During a 2013 segment with the *Hollywood Reporter* Roundtable, Washington explained, "After I did *Save the Last Dance*

I had to stop substituting in high schools because they were like, 'Chenille is substituting!'"[4]

Washington worked in television for the rest of 2001 and returned to the big screen with the role of Julie in Joel Schumacher's action and adventure comedy *Bad Company*. The movie centers on the aimless twin brother of a CIA agent who is recruited to complete a dangerous, top-secret mission. Chris Rock plays both twins, and Kerry Washington is Julie, girlfriend of Jake Hayes, the newly recruited agent. While the film was not well received by critics or at the box office, it does enjoy the distinction of being the last major production to film inside the World Trade Center before the September 11, 2001, attacks that destroyed the twin towers.

Television

Kerry Washington got her start in television performing in *ABC Afterschool Specials* in 1994. Two years later, she performed in the educational arts series *Standard Deviants*, a program that used sketch comedy and humor to teach a variety of school subjects. Washington would return to television in 2001 with roles on a variety of shows, some more widely viewed than others. She was cast as Maya Young, a witness to the shooting of a police officer, in the eighth season of the police drama *NYPD Blue*. Washington also appeared in an episode of the short-lived television show *Deadline* that featured Oliver Platt as a cursing, hard-drinking tabloid journalist. Washington played the role of Tina Johnson in an episode entitled "The Undesirables." She also appeared in an episode of *Law & Order* in 2001, where she portrayed a rapper's girlfriend who witnesses a shooting at a nightclub. The episode is entitled "Three Dawg Night" and also features Idris Elba playing an employee working at the nightclub at the time of the shooting. Kerry Washington also worked on A&E's original series *100 Centre Street* in 2001. The show centered on Manhattan's night court, detailing the lives of judges, lawyers, and criminals who pass through the judicial system. Kerry Washington appeared in several episodes of the show's 2001 season.

Washington would do television intermittently in the following years. In 2002, she was chosen for the role of Drea Westbrook, a client, on an episode of the CBS law drama *The Guardian*. In 2004, Washington portrayed the role of Mahandra McGinty in a pilot for the television series *Wonderfalls*. The pilot would go unaired even though the series was eventually picked up without Washington among the final cast. The same year, Washington was featured in the HBO television film *Strip Search*, which parallels several different stories concerning the intersection of personal freedoms and national security in the aftermath of 9/11. The HBO project was somewhat controversial and would only air once.

Washington's early television career was hit or miss, and while she was featured on some very popular television dramas, lasting success on television would elude her for years. Washington's early roles for which she is best remembered were on the big screen.

A Leading Woman Emerges

In the years after *Save the Last Dance*, Kerry Washington continued to perform in major motion pictures alongside Hollywood's top actors. In 2003, she had a small part in the movie *The United States of Leland*. The film explores the impact that a violent crime has on the lives of those involved. Ryan Gosling, Don Cheadle, and Kevin Spacey star in the film, which received mixed reviews. Later that year Washington appeared in *The Human Stain*, another intense drama starring Sir Anthony Hopkins and Nicole Kidman. Also in 2003, Washington was in *Sin*, a film starring Ving Rhames and Gary Oldman. Washington plays Kassie, the sister of Rhames's Eddie Burns, a retired homicide cop. When Kassie is assaulted, Eddie is forced out of retirement and into a twisted revenge plot enacted by a mysterious rival. In 2004, the movie *Against the Ropes* told the fictionalized story of the first successful female American boxing manager, Jackie Kallen. The film starred Meg Ryan and Omar Epps, with Kerry Washington playing a small part. *Against the Ropes* was a failure at the box office, but Washington was working regularly, making a living as a professional actor.

Washington returned to independent film in 2004 as Rosalie in *Sexual Life*, a comedy-drama revolving around the romantic **entanglements** of eight Los Angeles city

Kerry Washington and Omar Epps in 2004's *Against the Ropes*

dwellers. Washington had a more prominent role in this film and went on to star in Spike Lee's independent comedy *She Hate Me*, alongside Anthony Mackie. Mackie plays the role of John Henry "Jack" Armstrong, a wealthy executive who is accused of securities fraud and has his assets frozen. Washington plays Fatima Goodrich, Jack's ex-fiancée who came out as a lesbian after they broke up and now wants to have a baby. As a way of maintaining his expensive lifestyle, Jack accepts a large sum of money from Fatima and her girlfriend in exchange for impregnating them both. The movie follows Jack as he makes his living by offering his services to lesbians and deals with his legal troubles. The film parallels Jack Armstrong's struggles with those of Frank Wills, the security guard who alerted police

The Challenge of Being a Frog

Kerry Washington brings life to complex and diverse characters partly because she approaches her roles with the mind of a social scientist. As a child, Washington was interested in fields like psychology and education, and she went on to double major in anthropology and sociology at George Washington University. In May of 2013, she was chosen to give the commencement speech at her alma mater. Washington explained that she focused her classroom studies in the social sciences, but she also took acting classes. As a recipient of a presidential scholarship, she was required to audition for every single production at the Department of Theater and Dance. In 1996, Washington's junior year of college, the production was an environmental-themed musical called *Croak (The Last Frog)*. Washington has discussed how the role was terrifying to her because she was worried about the role being too difficult and concerned that she would not be able to do the physicality of a frog justice. After auditioning and getting the role of lead frog, Washington went about studying for her role like a social scientist. "I went to the zoo ... and I spent hours watching frogs. I read about frogs, I held frogs, I watched frog documentaries," Washington explained.[5] She worked to ensure that she could embody her character without her frog physicality seeming cartoonish. She explained that the role changed her thinking about how she uses her body and that her performance in the role is still her father's favorite performance.

to the break-in at Watergate during Nixon's presidency. Wills struggled with unemployment and poverty after exposing the national scandal. The film was very controversial, but it afforded Washington her first starring role in a major motion picture.

With every film since *Save the Last Dance*, Washington became a more and more well-known face in Hollywood productions. By the end of 2004, Washington would appear in an Oscar-winning major motion picture and open the door to more high-profile roles. In October of 2004, *Ray*, a movie following the life and times of music legend Ray Charles, opened to mostly positive reviews. It managed to bring in $125 million. Washington played Ray Charles's second wife, Della Bea Robinson, in the film. It was nominated for many different awards, and Jamie Foxx, who played Ray Charles, received the 2005 Academy Award for Best Actor. Kerry Washington's performance was also lauded by critics, and *Ray* became a must-see motion picture.

The successes of *Ray* fueled Washington's rising star and cemented her place as a serious actress who could help carry a major film. In the years that followed, Hollywood would begin to realize Washington's potential as a leading woman.

CHAPTER THREE

Entry into the Public Eye

By 2005, Kerry Washington had been in a wide variety of roles on television shows and in independent films, as well as in major motion pictures. Seven years out of college, Washington was creating a career as a professional actor. After the success of 2004's *Ray*, Washington continued to appear in a variety of independent projects and began to receive more work from major studio films. She continued to appear on television and began to get **recurring** roles.

A Good Year

In early 2005, *Ray* was one of the biggest movies in America. In February, the Academy Award for Best

Kerry Washington smiles at *Vanity Fair*'s 2005 Oscar party.

Actor went to Jamie Foxx for his deft portrayal of Ray Charles. Meanwhile, episodes of David E. Kelley's legal dramedy *Boston Legal* were airing on ABC. Washington had a recurring role as Chelina Hall, a lawyer from Texas who seeks help when a past outburst in court could jeopardize a client's future. Washington appeared in five episodes of *Boston Legal*, most of which aired in the spring of 2005, toward the end of the show's first season. That summer, Washington was attached to two different blockbusters. The first was *Mr. & Mrs. Smith*, which was released in June. It was the film that brought Brad Pitt and Angeline Jolie (Brangelina) together as John and Jane Smith, a couple of assassins working for competing agencies that are assigned the task of killing each other. Washington plays the role of Jasmine, sidekick to Jolie's Jane. *Mr. & Mrs. Smith* opened to mixed reviews but did well at the box office, earning around $478 million worldwide. In July, the superhero flick *Fantastic Four* was released, which featured Washington in the role of Alicia Masters. In the 2005 film, Masters becomes the love interest of Ben Grimm, whose fiancée leaves him after his transformation into The Thing. *Fantastic Four* did not fare well with the critics but it was a box office success. Its gross income worldwide was more than $330 million.

In addition to a recurring role on a major television show and supporting roles in two summer blockbusters, Washington also performed in a short film called *Wait* in 2005. The film also featured the work of actors Anna

Chlumsky and Tyson Beckford. Even as Washington became a more successful, high-profile actress, she remained invested in smaller independent projects as well.

Independent and Short Films

After *Wait*, Kerry Washington appeared in the independent film *The Dead Girl*, directed by Karen Moncrieff. A host of talented actors worked in the film, including Marcia Gay Harden, Mary Steenburgen, Josh Brolin and others. The movie is separated into five different segments. Washington appears in two segments as Rosetta, a sex worker and former roommate of the dead girl found in the beginning of the film. In preparation for the role, Washington spoke with New York City prostitutes and asked for their input on her character. *The Dead Girl* ran for only two weeks in the United States, but it was generally well received. In the end, it earned over $900,000, though much of that was earned overseas.

In 2007, Washington appeared in the short drama *Put It in a Book*, a film about two brothers torn apart by gang violence and the resulting choice between righteousness and revenge. *Put It in a Book* was one of the first films produced from the Make a Film Foundation, an organization that works to help critically ill youth realize their dreams of making short films. Make a Film Foundation supported *Put It in a Book* and Jabril Muhammad's dream of starring in his own short film.

Actor Michael Ealy and director Rodrigo García also worked on *Put It in a Book*.

Continued Success

In 2006, Washington appeared in the Wayans brothers' film *Little Man*. The off-the-wall comedy follows the exploits of a very short conman and his partner. They decide to pass the conman off as a baby on the doorstep of a couple wanting a child. Washington played the role of Vanessa Edwards, one-half of the childless couple. The film received generally negative press but was able to make more than $101 million in profit worldwide. In January of 2007, the fictionalized political thriller *The Last King of Scotland* opened in American theaters. The film is based on the Giles Foden novel and concerns the rule of Ugandan president Idi Amin. Washington portrays Kay Amin, a young wife of Forest Whitaker's Idi Amin. The film was widely praised by critics, and Forest Whitaker won the Academy Award for Best Actor for his portrayal of Idi Amin. The movie grossed more than $48 million worldwide.

After *The Last King of Scotland*, another comedy featuring a performance from Washington hit theaters with Chris Rock's *I Think I Love My Wife*. The comedy that Chris Rock wrote along with Louis C. K. was also directed and produced by Rock. The movie follows the temptation of Richard Cooper (played by Chris Rock), a happily married professional who sometimes fantasizes

Kerry Washington appears opposite James McAvoy in *The Last King of Scotland.*

about other women but never acts on his fantasies. One day an attractive woman from his past resurfaces, testing Cooper's resolve. Washington plays Nikki Tru, Cooper's temptress. *I Think I Love My Wife* was the second time Washington and Rock had worked together, the first being *Bad Company. I Think I Love My Wife* received generally negative reviews but made about $13 million worldwide in theaters and made an additional $13 million in DVD sales.

In June of 2007, the American public got to see Washington **reprise** her role as Alicia Masters in *Fantastic Four: Rise of the Silver Surfer.* The film continues to follow the Fantastic Four as they confront the Silver Surfer. It grossed $289 million but received negative reviews from critics. Originally there was supposed to be a third Fantastic Four film that would have explored the character of Alicia Masters and her relationship with Ben Grimm (The Thing), but it was subsequently canceled. Washington's role as Alicia Masters is especially significant because the part originally called for a blond-haired, blue-eyed actress, so Washington won the role on merit.

In early 2008, Washington returned to television with a guest appearance in the original USA detective comedy series *Psych*. In the eleventh episode of the second season, entitled "There's Something About Mira," Washington played the role of Mira Gaffney, Gus's secret wife who needs help finding her new fiancée who has gone missing.

Washington's next project to be released was a role in the film *Miracle at St. Anna*, directed by Spike Lee. The film was a screen **adaptation** by author James McBride of his 2003 novel. *Miracle at St. Anna* follows the story of four African American soldiers who seek refuge in a Tuscan village and bond with the inhabitants. Washington played the role of a lawyer hired to represent a suspected murderer. The movie is set in 1980s New York, with the action iterated through flashbacks to German-occupied Europe during the Second World War, making it a historical drama, decidedly outside of Lee's typical wheelhouse. This was the second time Washington got to work with director Spike Lee; their first film together was the 2004 comedy *She Hate Me*. *Miracle at St. Anna* was not well received by critics and

did not do well at the box office, grossing just over
$9 million. The film saw some controversy when it
was released in Italy as some Italians saw the film as
historically inaccurate. However, Lee did receive some
recognition for working so far outside his comfort zone.

Washington's next role to hit theaters would
challenge her to engage with complex racial dynamics as
the wife in an interracial couple tormented by a resident
of their new neighborhood who seems to be unhappy
with their relationship. Patrick Wilson performed
opposite of Washington in the movie, *Lakeview Terrace*,
while Samuel L. Jackson played their new neighbor, a
Los Angeles Police Department (LAPD) detective. The
plot is loosely based on a real-life series of events that
took place in Altadena, California. The real-life couple
was John and Mellaine Hamilton, and the LAPD officer
was Irsie Henry. The events were **chronicled** in local
newspapers. Washington was excited to take the role,
as the character was familiar to her but not the kind of
person likely to be seen on the big screen. She explained
in an interview:

> One thing was that I have never really seen this kind of
> African American woman onscreen before. She's a very
> modern character in that she's a crunchy-granola Berkeley
> graduate, progressive, environmentalist, open-minded, lives
> a really inclusive, multicultural lifestyle ... I have so many
> girlfriends like that, and my life is like that, and I thought,

"How great to have that woman onscreen." Because we tend in Hollywood to put people in a box—sometimes, not always … The other thing that really struck me when I read the script was this idea of the abuse of power … I think a big part of what the film is about is that you think you understand something and you may not. [Characters] think they know each other because of race, [or] I think I know who my husband is, but he's out in the car [secretly] smoking cigarettes … We think [Jackson's character] is just this racist, conservative cop who is harassing us, and then we find out this deeper plot point.[1]

While the film sought to explore a variety of social issues, it was not well received by all. While some critics like Roger Ebert gave the film glowing reviews, others thought it fell flat. *Lakeview Terrace* made over $44 million in theaters and an additional $22 million when it was released on DVD.

By 2009, Washington had been working in film for nine years and was enjoying a steady stream of varied roles. From television comedies to short independent films, Washington brought her chameleon talents to many different projects. She had successfully played a blind sculptor in the action superhero film *Fantastic Four* and Ray Charles's long-suffering second wife, Della Bea Robinson. She also explored interracial tensions with her role in *Lakeview Terrace*. Washington had to fight for her next role, which would challenge her more than

Washington surveys the neighborhood in the film *Lakeview Terrace*.

any of her previous projects. *Life Is Hot in Cracktown* is based upon the 1993 short story collection by Buddy Giovinazzo, who also directed the film. The stories are intense portrayals of the effect crack cocaine has on the lives of Manhattan neighbors. Washington plays the role of Marybeth, a transgender woman who does sex work to pay for surgery. Washington explained how she learned about the role, and her fight for it, in an interview with *Advocate* magazine:

> It's one of those really funny, weird, I guess hopefully meant-to-be situations. I had an agent who fell in love with the project. She encouraged me to read it and I read it and was terrified. I sort of have a history of saying that I'm drawn to work that challenges me. I have, unfortunately,

*said that publicly a lot. So she sent me on this interview
and I went to meet with Buddy [Giovinazzo, the director,]
feeling a bit nervous and ambivalent and not really sure
what he wanted to do but knowing that I was really drawn
to the writing. He was very honest with me and said that
he wasn't sure that I could do it. He really wanted for
Marybeth to be a realistic trans woman and that he didn't
want to distract from the argument—could this woman
really be a trans woman? Having me play the role he
thought might cost the film some of its authenticity, which
clearly is the most important part of the film.*

*So he actually ended up writing me the most beautiful
rejection letter I have ever received in my life. I forwarded it
to my agent and thought, My God. If ever I have to hear
no, this is the way to hear it. But it's that thing—when you
can't have it, then you really want it.*[2]

Washington was once again inspired to rise to the
challenge for a complex role and set about doing research
for it. She sought out help from books and movies, but
her most valuable insight came from a member of the
trans community, Valerie Spencer.

*I had an incredible woman named Valerie Spencer, who
was my transgender authenticity consultant. She was a girl
from the community and an incredible woman. I knew that
I was going to need a lot of support on this. So, I worked
with her and did a lot of reading, research, and watched
a lot of movies. I always work that way—I feel my job in*

some ways is that of an anthropologist to immerse myself into the world of the character. I knew this world was so different than mine so I had Valerie on set every day. I believe very strongly in a community of guidance. My job is to respect the community I am portraying.[3]

Washington's next project to reach audiences was *Mother and Child*, which premiered at the 2009 Toronto International Film Festival. Rodrigo García, the same director that Washington had worked with in the short film *Put It in a Book*, directed the film. *Mother and Child* tells the stories of several different women and their experiences of being a mother and/or a child. Washington plays the role of Lucy, a young baker who is seeking motherhood through adoption because she is unable to have children of her own. Washington describes her interest in the project and the character's journey in the film:

Actually, what appealed to me was the character and the challenge of playing this woman who goes through this incredible journey and evolution. These three women do that, and often in film you don't get that as a woman— we usually get to be the person who holds hands with the person who has a journey ... We meet [Lucy] at a time in her life where, up until now, pretty much everything has gone her way. She's got the perfect little husband and the bakery and the pearls, and suddenly she's faced with a

Washington (*right*) and Shareeka Epps in the film *Mother and Child*

situation she can't control. So a lot of what I think the film is about is watching a person learn how to let go of control. We watch her surrender not by choice but because the rug gets pulled out from her. And the person we see at the end of the film has really learned to live life on life's terms, in a wholly different way.[4]

David Alan Grier (*left*), James Spader (*center*), and Washington (*right*) shared the stage in the play *Race*.

The film, which also features performances by Naomi Watts, Samuel L. Jackson, and Annette Bening, received mostly positive reviews and won the Grand Prix du Jury at the 2010 Deauville American Film Festival.

Washington would enjoy another milestone role that year with a performance on Broadway in David Mamet's play *Race*. Washington played the role of Susan, a young attorney who works with a white colleague on the criminal defense of a wealthy man accused of a racially charged sex crime. Like *Lakeview Terrace*, *Race* explores the way we think about race. Washington also shared the stage with James Spader and David Alan Grier. The David Mamet production allowed Washington to fulfill her childhood dream of performing in a Broadway show.

After the success of 2004's dramatic biopic *Ray*, Washington continued to pursue a variety of roles that showed a wide range of talents. She spent the next six years filling her resume with characters who struggled with drugs, infertility, and violence. She brought her

A Reflection on the Black Panther Movement

After Washington's role in the Broadway play *Race*, she worked on another complex role, examining the life of a former Black Panther in Philadelphia working as a civil rights attorney on behalf of her former fellow Panthers. *Night Catches Us* blends fictional elements with the historical backdrop of the black power movement; it opens with archival footage of the Black Panthers and then moves into 1976. Director Tanya Hamilton was especially excited to see the project that she worked ten years to finish finally reach audiences. Washington plays Patricia, the widow of a slain Black Panther whose death draws a former cohort back to the neighborhood to pay his respects. In a 2010 interview with the *Root*, Washington explained how she viewed this role in relation to past characters that she had portrayed:

> I'm often really drawn to characters whose humanity other people may not be so quick to see. I often play women who people would be quick to judge or put in a box—like the wife of a famous person who stays even though he's cheating, or the wife of an African dictator who's one of five wives, or a transsexual, drug-addict prostitute. This was such a great opportunity to explore who the woman is who devotes her life to [the Black Panther] movement—not only who she is in the movement, but who she is ten years after the movement.[5]

Washington explored the 1970s Black Panther movement and its aftermath in *Night Catches Us*.

Anthony Mackie played the role of Marcus, who shares a simmering attraction to Patricia. The Philadelphia hip-hop band the Roots also participated in the project by scoring the film. It premiered at the 2010 Sundance Film Festival and received rave reviews.

charisma to television comedy and continued to work on independent projects even as her public profile rose. In the coming years, Washington would continue to play diverse characters in **landmark** productions. She would once again explore both comedy and dramatic films, working with such stars as Eddie Murphy, Tobey Maguire, and Quentin Tarantino. In addition to major motion pictures, Washington would explore television and land what has become the most **iconic** role of her career.

CHAPTER FOUR

A Shining Star

B y 2010, Kerry Washington had been in a myriad of productions from Broadway to short film. Her ever-changing résumé featured roles that were layered and complex, dramatic and comedic. As Washington's acting résumé continued to grow more and more diverse, she also began working in a role that would define her career and make her a true leading woman in her own television drama.

A Well-Rounded Career Continues

In 2010, Washington got the opportunity to participate in the film adaptation of an important one-of-a-kind theater project. Ntozake Shange's acclaimed piece *for colored girls*

Washington (*far right*) played a supporting role in *Mr. & Mrs. Smith* alongside Rachel Hunter, Theresa Barrera, and Michelle Monaghan.

who have considered suicide / when the rainbow is enuf is a series of lyrical poems performed with **choreographed** movement and music. The women performing each poem are only identified by color (the lady in orange, the lady in green, etc.). With its unconventional approach, the dramatic form tells the stories of seven different women dealing with racism and sexism.

The show was first performed in California, but in July of 1975, Shange moved the production to New York, about six months after its debut. Initially, performances took place in alternative theaters in downtown New York City. The show's growing popularity, especially among African American and Latino audiences, fueled its rise. In September of 1976, it opened at the Booth Theatre on Broadway and stayed until July of 1978 with a total of 742 performances. The piece was reimagined as a book and a television adaptation before Tyler Perry voiced an interest in making a film version in 2009. When asked how she came to be involved in the project Washington relayed this **anecdote**:

> I had sort of heard a rumor that [Perry] had the material, that he was going to be doing the film, and I cornered him at an event in New York and said, "What's going on? What are you doing? Is it true? What's happening?" At the time, he was really deep into a rewrite and didn't really want to talk about it, and I said, "Okay, fine, but I would really like to be a part of it," and then I got the call a few months later. He really wanted me to play the role of Kelly.[1]

The film adaptation of the play, called *For Colored Girls*, differed in that the roles of the women were named, and some were more closely based on poems from the original stage production than others. Washington got to perform alongside such great actresses as Thandie Newton, Janet Jackson, Whoopi Goldberg, Phylicia Rashad, Loretta Devine, and Anika Noni Rose. Washington talked with MTV about the responsibility of reimagining such a well-known production and what it was like to work with the other actresses in the film:

> *There was pressure, but I would call it more responsibility. There was sort of an excitement around the responsibility that we were taking on. So that was really how we walked into it. We weren't afraid of it per se. We wanted to honor the legacy of the work. If anything, we were inspired by each other ... One of the things that was so interesting about doing the film was that we all had such different processes. Some people really wanted to stay in character all the time. Other people asked to be called by their real names between every take because they felt they needed to be grounded in reality in that way. So I really commend Tyler for being able to take this group of actresses, who each work in such varied ways, and to still somehow get these incredible performances out of each of us.*[2]

Washington expressed gratitude for the opportunity to be involved in a film that chronicles black experience and acknowledged Tyler Perry's success and his unique **niche** in Hollywood storytelling.

In the beginning and end, I felt very grateful to and for Tyler, because who else could have done it? The amount of creative capital he's built in this industry has allowed him to be the person that could make this happen. And thank God that he has the emotional intelligence to do it right and be a collaborator, I never thought, "Oh gosh, he's a man and he won't get it" but who else would come to this story telling it this way unless they were committed? From beginning to end I felt grateful that we live in a time where we could do this production with this man. When we go work in our studios in LA, you shoot in the Greta Garbo theater and the Charlie Chaplin stage, and you're very grateful to be a part of that show biz legacy, but for this movie we went to his studio in Atlanta to shoot at [Tyler's] studio, and you're working on the Sidney Poitier stage in the Ruby Dee and Ossie Davis stage, and you realize the immense power that's been cultivated by him. What he's created was so beautiful in that we can actually own our stories and present them to the world in a place that comes from us. It's such an honor.[3]

The film opened to mixed reviews, with some critics believing that the movie version of the stage play fell short. Others praised the film as Perry's best work to date. In either case, the film was nominated for and won several accolades with African American film organizations.

Washington once again turned to comedy in her next two movies. The first was 2012's *A Thousand Words*, an Eddie Murphy comedy that centers on Jack McCall, a fast-talking literary agent who has a habit of stretching the truth (played by Murphy). After making a deal with a spiritual **guru**, Jack notices a bodhi tree in his yard and finds out that each time he speaks a word, a leaf falls from the plant. Since he will die once every leaf falls, he is forced to choose his words carefully. Washington portrays Jack's wife, Caroline, who thinks his newfound silence is a result of a lack of affection. Viewers watch as Jack struggles to communicate as his limited words cost him in his marriage and his professional life. Reviews were generally negative, and the film only made around $22 million, but Washington was excited to finally work with Eddie Murphy. In interviews, she talked about why she had looked forward to doing a film with Murphy:

> *It was particularly fun for me because I had worked with so many people who looked up to Eddie [and] who had been inspired to go into the business by him, from Chris Rock to Jamie Foxx to the Wayans Brothers. So, it was like finally going to the source ... He's very funny. But he's also incredibly focused, and takes comedy very seriously, if that makes any sense.*[4]

The dark comedy *The Details*, which was released in November of 2012, was Washington's next movie. In this twisted suburban jest, Jeff Lang (played by Tobey Maguire) discovers pests on his property, and his work to get rid of them sets off a chain reaction of deceit and violence. Washington plays Rebecca Mazzoni, the wife of Jeff's best friend. Critics found the film underwhelming, but by the time *The Details* was released in theaters, Washington was beginning to enjoy success as a leading woman in her own television series.

A Scandalous Dream Role

In April and May of 2012, the first season of ABC's *Scandal* aired, with Washington in the starring role as Olivia Pope. Pope is a Washington "fixer" who works with a team to neutralize scandals that their clients are involved in. Simultaneously, there is scandal within the team and in Pope's personal life. The show has a rapid pacing and has attracted a wide array of fans, including celebrities like Lena Dunham, the creator of HBO's *Girls*, and singer Mary J. Blige. Both have expressed their fondness for the show via Twitter, a favorite medium for viewers to share their take on the show's fast-paced twists. President Bill Clinton has also admitted to being a fan of the show.

As of mid-2017, the show had gone through six seasons, with the seventh slated to be its last. Washington was initially unsure about the project, even though Shonda Rhimes, the creator of such television magic as *Grey's Anatomy* and *Private Practice*, created it. Washington was much more focused on film acting when her agent suggested reading the television drama's script. She told the *Guardian*:

> *I thought, a network TV drama? No way, no way. I have a thriving film career ... But then I read the* Scandal *script and I was like, "Oh, I'm screwed. This is so good." Then I got really scared, because I did feel like it was written for me; you know, in some divine way, this was mine. But there were fifteen other actresses who felt the same. Shonda auditioned everyone and their mother, because for African American actresses this was the glass slipper—so she let everyone try it on.*[5]

Despite other powerhouse actresses such as Gabrielle Union and Taraji P. Henson auditioning for the role of Olivia Pope, Washington's audition earned her the iconic part. In subsequent interviews, Washington explained how the writing of the show got her excited to play the role.

> *The thing I first loved about the script was, you have this woman who's kind of larger than life in the public sphere. She's Olivia Pope; she's everything you've heard; she doesn't believe in crying. And yet by the end of the pilot episode, she's alone in a coat closet crying over her very personal scandal. That dichotomy of both power and vulnerability and confusion, that was what really drew me to her.*[6]

Pope's complex interplay of strength and vulnerability encouraged Washington to make less space in her schedule for acting in movies in order to accommodate the filming of a network television show. After filming the first season, Washington saw that acting in a well-written television show allowed for a prolonged immersion in character. She told *Backstage*:

> In a film, I may be playing multiple layers in a fully realized character over the course of two-and-a-half hours. In that case, I've done nine movies [with Scandal]. The writers are bringing such complicated, rich material that you have to keep unpeeling the layer of the character, which is so fulfilling and challenging. I'm still discovering who she is as the writer gives me more information. This job is just so much more fulfilling than anything I would have prayed for.[7]

Scandal quickly became a staple on ABC's Thursday-night programming and has made Kerry Washington instantly recognizable. Olivia Pope has a keen sense of style and has contributed to Washington being seen as something of a style icon. Though Washington has wrestled with Olivia Pope's moral leanings, she has become somewhat synonymous with the high-powered crisis manager. In an interview, Washington draws the line at calling Pope, someone personally embroiled in adulterous, political, and violent scandals, a model for behavior: "She's an entrepreneur, she's very smart, she has

Washington promotes a new season of the hit series *Scandal*.

The Real Olivia Pope

The hit ABC television series *Scandal* owes its huge success not just to its creator, Shonda Rhimes, and its lead actress, Kerry Washington, who shines as Olivia Pope. Rhimes based the role off of real-life crisis manager Judy Smith. Smith, who is also an African American woman, worked for President George W. Bush and has handled crisis situations for a myriad of public figures from Kobe Bryant to Monica Lewinsky.

Washington has a regular conference call with Smith before filming each episode in order to get input on how to make the scandals believable and what Smith's approach would be to solving specific conflicts. In fact, *Scandal* has leaned on the advice and experience of Smith throughout the production of the show. Smith explains how she helped Rhimes cultivate the character of Olivia Pope:

> Before the pilot, we spent a lot of time together— like a year—and they got to know what I do for a living. Shonda clearly has a sense for what I do. They've taken this high-stakes, chaotic, hectic feel of crisis communications and have done a great job of dramatizing it for television. It's incredible. My day-to-day stuff ... you can't obviously get it in an hour. But the beautiful thing about *Scandal* is it allows you to look at any crisis; it could be an entertainment crisis, a sports crisis, a political crisis, a legal crisis—it could be *any* crisis.[8]

Judy Smith is the real-life inspiration for Olivia Pope.

an amazing closet, and those are all things that I think are worthy of admiration. But she is nobody's role model."[9]

Since starting work on *Scandal*, Washington has made a concerted effort to focus on the show while doing a few movies when she has time in her schedule. Audiences have thoroughly enjoyed each season of *Scandal* while Washington continues to dazzle in major motion pictures.

While Washington was enjoying the success of her first season of work on a successful television drama, she was also preparing for another part. The talented actress would make her return to the big screen playing a supporting role in an anticipated Quentin Tarantino film alongside a familiar face from her past.

Reunited with Jamie Foxx

On Christmas Day 2012, American audiences got to see Washington perform in the Quentin Tarantino film *Django Unchained*. She appears as Broomhilda von Shaft, the wife of Django, played by Jamie Foxx, who played her on-screen husband in *Ray* previously. The project required Washington, playing an enslaved woman in need of rescue, to learn German and be on the receiving end of on-screen torture scenes. The film took a grueling eight months to shoot, which exhausted the entire cast, including Washington. Despite the intense process, Washington spoke enthusiastically about the importance of the film:

One of our background actors was a pastor, and he was saying on set that we are the answer to their prayers—to the very people who walked on this land. Who we are today—because we can read, own property, vote, marry, have our children and our freedom—that we are the answer to their prayers, and that's why we are here to tell their story.[10]

Some critics criticized Tarantino for his **visceral** depictions of slavery, but *Django Unchained* was generally well received. The film made a number of "Top Ten" lists and became Tarantino's highest-grossing film, earning over $425 million. Even criticism of the film's themes and images gave way to engaged scholarly dialogue and analysis.

After twelve years of appearing in a variety of entertainment mediums, Washington had cultivated a career playing an astonishing array of characters in a multitude of projects both big and small. In 2012, she began work on her most famous project, the ABC series *Scandal*. She has since reprised the role of Olivia Pope for several seasons and continues to appear in a variety of projects. Her most recent projects include working behind the scenes to foster developing talent.

CHAPTER FIVE

Activism

Kerry Washington's passions are not limited to the characters she portrays on-screen. Her politically conscious upbringing followed her into adulthood, and she has spoken and worked on a variety of causes. While Washington's family politics generally lean to the left, there was certainly room for disagreement between family members on issues. In a 2009 interview, she explained:

> *My family is very politically aware—dinner in my house has always been a place to discuss the sociopolitical realities of the world. As kids we were always encouraged to participate in those discussions ... I would say my mother is a lot more progressive than my dad. My mom is a teacher; my dad's a real estate broker who served time in the military. They're both definite, committed Democrats, but there's a wide range of ideas in my household and in my family.[1]*

Kerry Washington gives a riveting speech at the 2012 Democratic National Convention.

From politics to violence against women to issues of race and beauty, Washington has been engaged in a number of social causes and has shown her support through public appearances, fundraisers, and speeches. She has even served in a presidential administration.

Supporting Barack Obama

In 2008, Washington was recruited by Barack Obama's campaign to travel the country encouraging citizens to vote. Campaigning for Barack Obama's presidential election had a profound effect on Washington's identity as an American. She described what the experience offered her in a conversation with the *Advocate*:

It was pretty incredible. I guess I was really lucky, because I have this sort of hybrid personal history in that I grew up in the Bronx and then I went to Spence [an exclusive private school] in New York, so they realized very early on that they could send me to a tea for the ladies' society and they could send me to the historically black university and so, once I got on the road, that was it. Soccer clubs in the suburbs to black churches. I was covering every demographic possible. I was really excited to do it.

I went to parts of the country I've never been to before. I literally had never been to Tennessee, had never been to Arkansas, had never been to Texas, and so here I am, going to these places—and going deep into communities and meeting all different kinds of people from different socioeconomic backgrounds. It was just amazing and really, in a way, restored my faith in America.[2]

Michelle Obama and Kerry Washington walk with young students.

Barack Obama would, of course, go on to be elected to the presidency, much to the delight of Kerry Washington. Though the candidate she campaigned for was elected to the presidency, Washington's work with the Obama administration was not finished.

Arts Education

After Barack Obama was elected president, Kerry Washington was appointed to serve as a member of the President's Committee on the Arts and Humanities. Committee members are appointed for the term of the administration and are citizens who work in a variety of fields, including art, science, and government. Members focus on improving one of three areas: arts and humanities education, cultural exchange, or creative economy. At *Variety*'s 2013 Power of Women event, Washington talked a bit about how she came to serve on the committee:

> Barack Obama was the first candidate ever to run with the arts as part of his platform for his future presidency, so when I was on the trail as a surrogate for the campaign, I talked a lot with the campaign about the importance of the arts, and the National Endowment for the Arts, the National Endowment for the Humanities. So, once he was president, the administration really felt like it was a good match, so they reached out to me.[3]

During Washington's service, she worked toward improving arts and humanities education as an ambassador of the arts to Savoy Elementary School, an economically disadvantaged institution in Washington, DC. Since arts programming was introduced to Savoy, there has been a rise in math and reading scores, as well as an increase in enrollment and attendance. In May of 2013, First Lady Michelle Obama toured the school with Washington.

Washington represented the President's Committee on the Arts and Humanities at different speaking engagements and expressed how important arts education is to her. She said at the *Variety* Power of Women event:

Students dance the Lindy Hop with Kerry Washington.

It's really an honor to serve for the Obama administration in this capacity because I get to help protect the arts and bring the arts into the lives of young people that need it the most ... Our committee has had a signature focus on arts in education and making sure that the arts remain an important part of the curriculum.[4]

Though Washington's time working in a presidential administration has ended, she has maintained ties with an important organization. Washington continues to work as a TurnAround Artist with TurnAround Arts, an arts education institution led by the President's Committee on the Arts and Humanities. She works with Warren Lane Elementary School in Inglewood, California, where she takes part in student workshops, visits classrooms, and attends events to encourage student participation.

On the Road to Reelection

When Barack Obama began his bid for reelection in 2012, Kerry Washington was, of course, in his corner. Washington hit the campaign trail with the same passion she had in 2008. She even took her dad along on a few stops. In September of 2012, she talked to Essence.com about her plans leading up to the election. "You know, I had a great Father's Day this year because my dad and I went to a bunch of cities in central Florida and hit the campaign trail together. So I imagine I'll do more interviews and continue to encourage people between now and November to get out there and volunteer with your family."[5]

In addition to campaigning on the ground and talking about the election in interviews, Washington also wrote an article for the *Daily Beast* that expressed her support for Obama. In the article, she made the argument that Barack Obama was focused on supporting women and making sure their issues were confronted.

President Obama knows the importance of women's rights and women's health. He was raised by a single mom, and he has been surrounded by smart, strong women ever since—he's married to one and he's a father of two. So for our president, women's issues aren't just political, they're personal for him as well.

When President Obama made the Lilly Ledbetter Fair Pay Act the very first bill he signed—he did so because he believes the hard work of our daughters is just as important *as the work of our sons. He fought for Obamacare so women can access quality, affordable health care. He put two more women on the Supreme Court because he believes women should have an equal voice in the decisions being made at the highest levels of our democracy. And he knows we still have work to do.*[6]

That year, Washington was invited to make a speech at the Democratic National Convention. On the last night of the convention, Washington gave a rousing speech centered on the first words of the Constitution of the United States.

So many struggled so that all of us could have a voice in this great democracy and live up to the first three words of our constitution: We the people. I love that phrase so much. Throughout our country's history, we've expanded the meaning of that phrase to include more and more of us. That's what it means to move forward. And that's what this election is all about.

Look, I get it. Whether it's school, work, family, we've all got a lot on our minds. People say to me, "I'm just too busy to think about politics." But here's the thing: You may not be thinking about politics, but politics is thinking about you.

Today there are people trying take away rights that our mothers, grandmothers, and great-grandmothers fought for: our right to vote, our right to choose, affordable quality education, equal pay, access to health care. We the people can't let that happen.[7]

Barack Obama was able to win reelection. However, as the president's second term came to an end, Washington went back to work as a political surrogate, this time for Secretary of State Hillary Clinton.

Kerry Washington Was "With Her"

During the intense 2016 campaign season, Washington made it clear which candidate had her support. In March, she appeared in a campaign advertisement for Hillary Clinton along with producer Shonda Rhimes. Actresses Viola Davis and Ellen Pompeo from Rhimes's shows *How to Get Away with Murder* and *Grey's Anatomy* also made appearances.

Washington also participated in a live-streamed question and answer session at Twitter's headquarters in San Francisco with Hillary Clinton, alongside comedic actress Amy Poehler. Clinton was promoting her new book, *Hard Choices*, and she took questions from attendees and both actresses. Both Washington and Poehler asked about female empowerment, and Clinton gave advice to women who think they might enjoy public service. She also spoke to the importance of women finding confidence in their uniqueness. The former secretary of state also took the opportunity to let Washington know she was a fan, saying, "Isn't Kerry Washington terrific? I mean, really just a fabulous actress and a really good person."[8]

Washington had already endorsed the candidate on her Instagram when Clinton visited the set of *Scandal*.

Washington speaking at the 2017 Women's March in Los Angeles

Washington posted a photo of herself with the former secretary of state along with the caption, "A good friend came by set today. Proud to say … #imwithher."[9]

Aftermath of 2016 Election

Despite a hard-fought campaign, Hillary Clinton was not elected president of the United States. The morning after the election of Donald Trump, Washington noticed #OliviaPope trending on Twitter because people were looking for a savior. "This is not about Olivia Pope," Washington told the crowd, "This is not about anybody saving you, people! This is about you and me standing up for our democracy!"[10] Then the day after Donald Trump was inaugurated, Washington participated in the Women's March in Los Angeles and gave a rousing speech on the importance of participating in the democratic process.

In March of 2017, she echoed these sentiments in an interview with POPSUGAR:

Democracy doesn't work unless we participate. Participating means more than just voting. It's what we're seeing now: people going to town halls, and making phone calls, and sending post cards, and writing letters to your representatives to let them know—to remind them that they work for us. And the only way they can really work for us is if we remind them about the things we care about, and we show up, especially on voting days ... I really think participation in the process is the cause that's really important to me now. I'm sad that over half of our country didn't vote in the last election. It only works as "We the People" if "We the People" all have a seat at the table. If some of us silence ourselves by not showing up, or some of us allow ourselves to be silenced by voting rights laws that limit participation, then we're not able to really have our government represent who we are as a country.[11]

It's clear that regardless of who is seated in the Oval Office, Kerry Washington will continue to be involved, encouraging others to participate, working to make opportunities for the less fortunate, and fighting for causes she believes in.

Champion for Women

Not only has Kerry Washington worked to raise awareness of women's issues through her portrayals on-screen, she has been a passionate feminist activist off-screen. In fact, at times Washington has found ways to merge her passions for acting and fashion with her social justice activism.

V-Day

It was an inspiring theater production that first sparked Washington's interest in working to end violence against women. Washington explained to *People* magazine how seeing a fellow actress perform in an inspiring show made her want to contribute:

> *Back in 2000, I had just finished filming* Save the Last Dance, *and my friend and costar Julia Stiles invited me to watch her in Eve Ensler's play* The Vagina Monologues. *I was so moved by all these stories of women's identity, value and worth. After that I became part of the movement to end violence against women.*[12]

Eve Ensler's singular examination of sex, violence, and social **stigma** features a variety of different monologues performed by women about their bodies. The intimate and challenging performances inspired female audience members to share their own stories. In 1998, four years after the play saw its first audience, Ensler and a group of New York City women established V-Day, an organization that encourages participants to put on productions of *The Vagina Monologues* in February. The money raised by the performances goes to programs dedicated to stopping violence against women, such as rape crisis centers and shelters. While V-Day started with just one performance in New York City, nearly six thousand productions take the stage at annual V-Day events across the globe. Kerry Washington's first V-Day performance was in Harlem in 2002, and she has since performed in many other V-Day benefits. Washington also serves on V-Board, a group of women who help provide V-Day events guidance and support.

Combining Research and Advocacy

In 2006's haunting indie flick *The Dead Girl*, Kerry Washington plays Rosetta, a sex worker navigating a web of violence. In true fashion, Washington knew she would need to research the role in order for her performance to be authentic. Before filming, Washington and Eve Ensler performed a benefit at a halfway house run by Girls Educational and Mentoring Services, an organization dedicated to helping victims of sexual exploitation create new lives for themselves. Washington was able to get vital feedback from the women in attendance and learn what life on the street is really like. Their answers helped Washington grasp the challenges and dangers that her character faces in the movie. They also helped her better understand the close, interdependent relationship between Rosetta and Krista, another sex worker played in the movie by Brittany Murphy. Washington shared what she learned with Murphy, enhancing both of their performances on-screen.

Washington's dedicated investigation into the lives of those affected by sex work allowed her to approach the role of Rosetta with nuance and compassion. Washington also helped to publicize the work of Girls Educational and

Mentoring Services, whose founder, Rachel Lloyd, went on to receive the Reebok Human Rights Award in 2006.

Empowerment Through Fashion

Over the course of *Scandal*, viewers have marveled at the wardrobe of Olivia Pope. From her killer stilettoes to that flawless white coat, Pope's fashion sense is often mentioned in the same breath as the show's frenetic pacing and twists. While Washington professes to be less of a fashionista than the high-powered crisis manager she plays on television, Washington has found a way to advocate for women through their clothing, accessories, and makeup.

In 2014, Washington partnered with the show's costume designer, Lyn Paolo, to create a line of clothing inspired by Olivia Pope's empowered style for The Limited. Washington relates how they went about capturing Pope's style:

> [We] wanted to create a way of dressing that embodied empowerment but was also feminine and womanly, a way that you could tell that someone was a woman and tell that she was powerful, and you didn't have to separate those two ideas.[13]

In 2014, Washington got another chance to design for a cause when the Allstate Foundation's Purple Purse program selected her as an ambassador. The program seeks to raise awareness of the financial implications of domestic abuse and the reality that women are often less

A Diversity of Options

While many celebrities act as spokespeople for different beauty brands and do little more than appear in advertisements, Washington has forged an important partnership with the skincare company Neutrogena. In 2013, she became a creative consultant with them. At the time, Neutrogena did not have a shade in its makeup line that was dark enough to match Washington's skin tone. Fans took to social media to voice their displeasure at Neutrogena for its lack of options. Eventually, Washington told fans that she would be working with the company to develop new shades for darker complexions. She commented, "When I first started out at Neutrogena, there was not a foundation for me, and there was actually some pushback about that online. I very purposefully did not address it [then], because I knew that I was about to engage in this labor of love."[14]

In 2016, Neutrogena released some new shades for darker skin tones. While promoting the new shades that she had helped develop, Washington shared her frustrations with the beauty industry: "I remember being a little girl at the drugstore with my mother, looking at stockings, and having a realization that when a package says 'nude,' they're not talking about me. That was traumatizing for me as a little girl."[15] Washington has also worked with OPI, a nail polish company, to produce her own line of colors. The colors have feminist names like "Madam President" and "We the Female." With a variety of product lines, Washington has been working to help all women feel included in the beauty industry.

Vicky Dinges (*left*), Kerry Washington (*center*), and Tom Wilson (*right*) at the 2014 Allstate Foundation Purple Purse Program.

able to leave a violent situation for monetary reasons. Washington designs a handbag each year, which is then auctioned off, with the proceeds going to a number of nonprofit organizations focused on stopping domestic violence across the country. By offering purple purses and purple purse charms to compassionate consumers, the Allstate Purple Purse program is hoping their purple accessories act as conversation pieces between women. In this way, the program is stemming the tide of domestic violence through financial support and fighting stigma by providing opportunities for dialogue.

Washington has pursued her passions not just onstage and on-screen but through advocacy. She has received recognition and awards for both her well-defined characters and her social presence. In the next stage of her career, Washington aims to continue accepting challenging roles and to spend more time behind the scenes, developing complex material into feature films and television.

CHAPTER SIX

Recognition and Future Plans

Kerry Washington has always been something of a chameleon on-screen. Her ability to totally inhabit the characters she plays allowed her to fly under the Hollywood radar in terms of celebrity. However, she garnered attention from film critics immediately. From *Save the Last Dance* to *Confirmation*, Washington's performances have earned her accolades, while fans respect her for her commitment to advocacy.

Recognition for Performances

In 2001, Washington had been out of college for three years when *Save the Last Dance*, her first major motion

Kerry Washington on the red carpet at the Academy Awards in 2016 picture, was released in theaters. The movie, about Sara, a white teen who moves to Chicago and finds herself in an interracial relationship, was an overwhelming hit among teen audiences. That year, the Teen Choice Awards nominated Washington for Choice Breakout Performance for her portrayal of Chenille, who befriends Sara. Washington went home with the award.

In 2002, the Independent Spirit Awards nominated Washington for her role in the independent production *Lift*. Washington plays a professional shoplifter with a dysfunctional family. She also got some attention from the Urbanworld Film Festival, a film festival that highlights diverse voices. That year, the festival chose to add an awards component to its event lineup with the MECCA (Minority Entertainment for the Cinematic and Creative Arts) Awards. The awards were implemented to recognize emerging and veteran entertainers who have blazed trails for the next generation of artists. Washington was honored with the MECCA Future of Film Award, an accurate prediction about where her career would go. In March of 2004, the Chlotrudis Society for Independent Film, a film society in Massachusetts, also recognized Washington's burgeoning film career. The society was initially impressed by Washington's work in the independent film *Our Song* and has been following her work since.

With the success of *Ray* in 2004, Washington found herself attending a number of awards ceremonies. The film won more than fifty awards and earned Jamie Foxx, Washington's costar and on-screen husband, an Academy Award and a Golden Globe. Washington shared in the recognition when she won the NAACP Image Award for Outstanding Actress in a Motion Picture for her work in the film.

Much of Washington's recognition has been overwhelmingly positive, but she has received some attention for an appearance that one awards show thought was particularly bad. The Golden Raspberry Awards, or Razzies, recognize the worst in motion pictures. In 2007, Washington shared the "award" for Worst Screen Couple with Shawn and Marlon Wayans for their movie *Little Man*. However, the Image Awards nominated Washington for Outstanding Supporting Actress in a Motion Picture for her work in *The Last King of Scotland* the same year.

While most of Washington's nominations have been the result of her work on the big screen, her work on television did not go unnoticed early in her career. In 2006, the Image Awards nominated her for her work on the television series *Boston Legal*. In 2008, the Online Film and Television Association nominated Washington for her role in the comedy *Psych*.

In 2000, the Foundation for the Augmentation of African Americans in Film (FAAAF) introduced its awards ceremony and fundraiser, the Black Reel Awards. Just two years after its inception, the Black Reel Awards recognized two of Washington's early performances. She was nominated for Best Independent Actor (for her role in *Lift*) as well as Best Supporting Actress (for *Save the Last Dance*) but did not win in either category. She was nominated again in 2005 and 2007 for *Ray* and *The Last King of Scotland* but again failed to take home top honors. In 2011, Washington was once again nominated for two performances: Best Supporting Actress for her work in the film *For Colored Girls* and Best Actress for *Night Catches Us*. She won Best Actress and took home her first Black Reel Award. The recognition must have been especially poignant for Washington. At the premiere of the film, she talked about basing her character portrayal on a special person in her life:

> *I'm sort of playing my mom in the film because she kind of has that position in the community. She was everybody's mom when I was growing up and she took care of everybody ... In a lot of ways I'm sort of doing an **homage** to my mom and the service that she's given to the Bronx and to New York.*[1]

The Foundation for the Augmentation of African Americans in Film recognized Washington once again in 2013 when she was nominated for her role in the Quentin Tarantino film *Django Unchained*. In February of 2017, Washington won her second Black Reel Award. This time she won in the category Outstanding Actress in a TV Movie or Limited Series for her work in the HBO film *Confirmation*.

In 2013, Washington was honored for her work in both *Django Unchained* and her television series *Scandal*. The show received the TV Guide Fan Favorite Award that year, which Washington shared with the cast and creator. Washington also secured her first Emmy nomination for *Scandal* in 2013. The Women's Image Network, a nonprofit that recognizes men and women in the media industry for making work that values girls and women, also honored Washington for her portrayal of Olivia Pope. She took home the award for Best Actress in a TV Drama Series, while Shonda Rhimes won for Best TV Show Written by a Woman, also for *Scandal*. The BET Awards chose Washington for Best Actress in 2013 and acknowledged her work in both *Django Unchained* and *Scandal*. The NAACP also paid homage to Washington with nominations for Outstanding Supporting Actress in a Motion Picture (*Django Unchained*) and Outstanding Actress in a Drama Series (*Scandal*). Washington took home the top awards in both categories and was also recognized for her work in public service with the President's Award. In her speech after winning for *Django Unchained*, she acknowledged the victims of slavery. "This award does not belong to me," Washington said. "It belongs to our ancestors. We shot this film on a slave plantation in the South. They were with us every step of the way."[2] A year later, she won Outstanding Actress in a Drama Series from the Image Awards for her work on *Scandal*.

Recognition for Activism

Washington has always tried to challenge herself when considering which roles to take. "I like to take risks for the good or the bad. I like to challenge myself and I like to do all different kinds of material ... It depends on the mood I'm in and it depends on what I did last and what seems like a challenge for me at that point in my life ... I kind of like to change it up."[3] A variety of advocacy organizations have recognized Washington for the humanity she invests in her characters and her willingness to breathe life into all different kinds of roles in such a variety of projects. In 2015, one of the largest gay rights organizations in America honored Washington for her representations of LGBT individuals on-screen.

The twenty-sixth annual Gay and Lesbian Alliance Against Defamation (GLAAD) Media Awards recognized Washington with the Vanguard Award, an honor bestowed upon media professionals who promote equality. Ellen DeGeneres presented the award to Washington, who made a moving speech about the power of inclusive storytelling:

I don't decide to play the characters I play as a political choice. Yet the characters I play often do become political statements. Because having your story told as a woman, as a person of color, as a lesbian, as a trans person, or as any member of any disenfranchised community, is sadly often still a radical idea. There is so much power in storytelling, and there is enormous power in inclusive storytelling, in inclusive representations. That is why the work of GLAAD is so important. We need more LGBT representation in the media. We need more LGBT characters and more LGBT storytelling. We need more diverse LGBT representation. And by that, I mean lots of different kinds of LGBT people living all different kinds of lives. And this is big—we need more employment of LGBT people in front of and behind the camera.

We can't say that we believe in each other's fundamental humanity, and then turn a blind eye to the reality of each other's existence, and the truth of each other's hearts. We must be allies and we must be allies in this business, because to be represented is to be humanized, and as long as anyone anywhere is being made to feel less human, our very definition of humanity is at stake, and we are all vulnerable. We must see each other, all of us. And we must see ourselves, all of us. And we have to continue to be bold and break new ground until that is just how it is, until we are no longer "firsts" and "exceptions" and "rare" and "unique." In the real world, being an "other" is the norm. In the real world, the only norm is uniqueness, and our media must reflect that. Thank you GLAAD, for fighting the good fight.[4]

Washington continues to focus her efforts on inclusive storytelling, but she is beginning to spend more time developing projects as a producer. A year after receiving GLAAD's Vanguard Award, Washington released an HBO TV movie about Anita Hill's controversial and

Kerry Washington (*left*) with Anita Hill, promoting the film *Confirmation*

landmark testimony at the confirmation hearing of Supreme Court nominee Clarence Thomas. Washington executive produced the TV movie and also starred as Anita Hill. The film highlighted the national conversation about sexual harassment that Anita Hill's testimony sparked. Washington won a Black Reel Award and earned nominations from the Emmys and the Golden Globes for her performance. While continuing to promote equality with the roles she takes, Washington has also begun to develop projects that allow for more inclusive storytelling.

Future Projects

While Washington has received a number of accolades for past performances and advocacy, she continues to forge into the future with new roles both in front of and behind the camera.

An Eye for Production

Washington's inspiration for *Confirmation* came from the 2013 documentary *Anita: Speaking Truth to Power*. After seeing it, Washington contacted Susannah Grant, the writer of *Erin Brockovich*, and Michael London, the producer of *Milk*, about making a movie that explores the testimony by showing the perspective of Hill but also Clarence Thomas and Joe Biden. (Biden was the chair of the Senate Judiciary Committee at the time of the hearing.) When she reached out to Grant and London, she said, "I don't want to be a figurehead of a producer. If we do this together, I really need to be a full producer."[5] In *Confirmation*, Washington got a chance to show fans that she is not just multitalented in terms of performance range but can also hold her own behind the scenes. After starring in the historical drama that she also executive produced, the actress started her own production company aimed at developing interesting, diverse new content.

A Seat at the Table

Shortly after the success of the HBO TV movie *Confirmation*, Washington formed Simpson Street Productions. Named after the street her mother grew up on, Simpson Street was created with the aim of developing inclusive content. When speaking to *Elle* magazine about the decision to start developing projects, Washington explained why she was drawn to the idea:

> At this point in my career, it felt important for me to be creating work for myself, and not, like, sitting at home and waiting to be invited to a party … I've been so lucky, and I want to make sure the level of work continues to be as good. So I thought, Maybe I should take a seat at the table and be part of the team that makes things happen, instead of putting my artistic destiny in other people's hands.[6]

Shortly after Washington created Simpson Street, she signed a two-year deal with ABC Studios. Washington was excited to announce the move and enthusiastic about partnering with the *Scandal* network.

I believe strongly in the importance of having a seat at the table, which makes starting this production company thrilling for me. It's an honor to be at a point in my career when I can help generate projects that are exciting, necessary, and truly reflect the world around us. I'm grateful to be on this journey with ABC, a network that remains unparalleled in its commitment to inclusive storytelling.[7]

During an appearance at the 2016 Women of Sundance brunch, Washington talked about her interest in producing and how she decides which work to pursue. "I look for work that makes us feel less alone, not by forcing us all to be part of one kind of hero's journey, but realizing that heroes come in many different shapes and sizes and hues and genders."[8]

Washington also spoke about the importance of expanding opportunities for women. She said, "A big part of it is the courage to say great, I'm so happy you've given me this deal, but I'm also going to hire another woman to help me run this company, and I'm also going to do a film about a woman, and I'm gonna hire an Academy Award–nominated woman to write it, and to just never accept that us being in the room alone is enough."[9] Washington went on to explain that she's looking forward to "hiring people of color, and hiring people that are part of the LGBTQ community, just making sure that people that we as a society have labeled as other have a seat at the table to be leaders, and to make the table look like what the real world looks like."[10]

Shortly after Simpson Street's deal with ABC Studios, it was announced that their first project would be a police drama called *Patrol*, focusing on four female LAPD officers who attended police academy together and are reunited to face a secret from their past. Washington announced she would executive produce the show. Another potential series to come out of the ABC Studios deal is *Melting Potts*, a family comedy that centers on a large, blended family that is "equal parts New Jersey, Indian, Muslim and Jewish."[11] Ryan Jaffe will write the series and will executive produce along with Washington and Sharla Sumpter Bridgett.

In addition to developing new content for television, Simpson Street also announced plans to develop three novels into feature films. One of the novels had not yet been released at the time of the announcement.

From the Page to the Screen

In early 2017, it was announced that TriStar had acquired the rights to develop a film based on *The Perfect Mother*, a novel by Aimee Malloy that was sold to HarperCollins, even though the book had not yet been published. The book focuses on a group of Brooklyn mothers who socialize together. One of the mothers' babies is abducted, and three new moms go to great lengths to find the child alive. Washington is expected to star in and produce the film.

It was announced in March of 2017 that Kerry Washington will also produce an adaptation of a *New*

York Times best seller. Nadia is the seventeen-year-old **protagonist** in Brit Bennett's debut novel, *The Mothers*, which is set in a Southern California town. Nadia begins dating Luke, the local pastor's son, and becomes pregnant. The novel follows Luke, Nadia, and her friend Aubrey in the aftermath of Nadia's decision about how to handle the pregnancy. The **omniscient** church "mothers" of the town narrate the novel. Bennett will also write the screenplay for the film version of her book. Warner Brothers will produce along with Simpson Street and Natalie Krinsky.

Simpson Street is also in talks to adapt Natalie C. Anderson's best-selling debut novel, *City of Saints and Thieves*. Universal Pictures has optioned the book, which follows Tina, a young girl in Kenya who is recruited by a gang of street kids after her mother's murder. While planning to **avenge** her mother, Tina realizes that she may not know the whole truth about her mother's death.

While Kerry Washington has enchanted audiences onstage and on film, she has begun to branch out and bring her passion for inclusive storytelling to producing complex content centered on women. Though Washington is attached to produce a handful of projects already, she will keep pursuing her first love—acting.

Another Milestone

Back in 2008, it was announced that Washington would participate in an animated series based on the Marvel Comic character Black Panther. The series was developed

Family First

With her role in *Cars 3*, Washington will finally be able to show her work to two very important people, her children, Isabelle and Caleb. "It's fun, the idea of doing something that the kids can actually enjoy," Washington said.[12] Washington is married to Nnamdi Asomugha, a former cornerback in the National Football League. The two wed in a quiet ceremony in 2013.

When asked about her pregnancy experience, Washington gushed to *InStyle*, "There's something about pregnancy … that willingness to take up more space in the world—that is liberating."[13] Washington's liberation would also pose an interesting problem on her hit show *Scandal*. Late into her pregnancy with her son Caleb, she was filming the sixth season. She and the crew had to find ways to hide Washington's pregnant belly. On *Good Morning America*, she joked about trying to conceal her pregnancy: "You could play a really fun game for the first five episodes of find the bump."[14] Luckily, she did not have to film the whole season with such **constraints**. After shooting five episodes, Washington gave birth.

Though she is often in the public eye, Washington is careful to keep her family life separate from her work. She tends not to discuss her family with the press. However, during a sit-down with the *Los Angeles Times*, she did share with fans how she felt about her career and her young family: "I just feel really blessed that I'm kind of living extraordinary dreams come true in my work life and in my personal life."[15]

for BET with Washington voicing the character Princess Shuri. The show never aired on television in the United States and was not released to American audiences until early 2011. In early 2017, it was announced that Washington would return to animation with a character in a major motion picture.

Disney's Cars series follows the adventures of Lightning McQueen, a sports car voiced by actor Owen Wilson. In March of 2017, Walt Disney Pictures announced that Washington would appear in *Cars 3* as a fast-talking red sports car named Natalie Certain. "She is a super-smarty-pants statistician. She reminds [me] of a statistical analyst on cable news or SportsCenter." Washington told *People*. "She knows everything there is to know about the ins and outs of statistics when it comes to racing."[16]

With new projects always on the horizon, Washington has a lot to look forward to. When asked about producing, Washington said, "I want to be able to contribute to how a story is told. Content is going through such an exciting shift. Content is taking on such a different structure, as is how we engage with it, and it's fun to be in that adventure."[17] Whether she is embodying characters on-screen or working behind the scenes to develop projects, or both, advocacy groups and audiences alike are excited to see where Washington's adventures take her.

2002

Plays the role of Julie in *Bad Company*.

2000

Washington appears in an independent film titled *Our Song*.

2005

Portrays Chelina Hall on the television series *Boston Legal*, Jasmine in *Mr. & Mrs. Smith*, and Alicia Masters in the Marvel film *Fantastic Four*.

1994

Washington acts in first television role in *ABC Afterschool Specials*.

2007

Reprises role of Alicia Masters in *Fantasic Four: Rise of the Silver Surfer* and appears in short film *Put It in a Book*.

Appears in the Wayans brothers comedy *Little Man*, *The Last King of Scotland*, and *The Dead Girl*.

Kerry Marisa Washington is born.

2006

1977

Appears in Spike Lee's *She Hate Me*, *Against the Ropes*, and *Ray*.

She graduates from George Washington University.

2004

She appears in *Save the Last Dance*, *Lift*, and several television series, including *Law & Order* and *NYPD Blue*.

1998

2001

2013

Marries Nnamdi Asomugha.

2010

Performs in the film *Night Catches Us* as well as Tyler Perry's *For Colored Girls*.

2008

Reunites with director Spike Lee in *Miracle at St. Anna*, plays Lisa Mattson in *Lakeview Terrace*, and appears on television series *Psych*.

Plays Marybeth in *Life Is Hot in Cracktown* and the role of Lucy in *Mother and Child*.

2009

Appears in Quentin Tarantino's *Django Unchained*, the Eddie Murphy film *A Thousand Words*, and the first season of *Scandal*.

2012

Washington has her first child, a daughter named Isabelle Amarachi.

2014

2016

She executive produces and stars in *Confirmation*, forms Simpson Street production company, and signs a two-year deal with ABC to develop content. She has her second child, a son named Caleb.

Disney announces Washington will play the role of Natalie Certain in *Cars 3*.

2017

SOURCE NOTES

Chapter 1

1. David Kamp and Jessica Diehl, "Ms. Kerry Goes to Washington: The First Lady of Scandal Speaks," *Vanity Fair*, August 2013, http://www.vanityfair.com/style/2013/08/kerry-washington-scandal-cover-story.

2. Elizabeth Kiefer, "Kerry Washington Talks Race, Sexual Harassment and Her New HBO Film, *Confirmation*," *Refinery29*, April 13, 2016, http://www.refinery29.com/2016/04/107679/kerry-washington-confirmation-interview.

3. Bodie Brizendine, "Moral Adventure," The Spence School, April 25, 2016, http://www.spenceschool.org/page/news-detail?pk=849666.

4. Beth Stevens, "What's Up, Kerry Washington? The *Race* Star on Mamet, Swearing and Kissing Kristin Chenoweth," Broadway, March 12, 2010, http://www.broadway.com/buzz/148420/whats-up-kerry-washington-the-race-star-on-mamet-swearing-and-kissing-kristin-chenoweth.

5. "Kerry Washington," Biography, January 31, 2017, http://www.biography.com/people/kerry-washington-21041523.

6. Jarett Wieselman, "Kerry Washington's Journey from Girl to Gladiator," BuzzFeed, January 31, 2014, https://www.buzzfeed.com/jarettwieselman/kerry-washingtons-journey-from-girl-to-gladiator?utm_term=.li7Ykrdoa#.uqAW8Pr7a.

7. Stevens, "What's Up, Kerry Washington?"

8. Decca Aitkenhead, "Kerry Washington: Notes on a Scandal," *Guardian*, June 28, 2013, https://www.theguardian.com/culture/2013/jun/28/kerry-washington-scandal-interview.

9. Lindsay Peoples, "Kerry Washington Explains Why She Refuses to Conform to Hollywood's Beauty Standards," *New York Magazine*, April 11, 2016, http://nymag.com/ thecut/2016/04/kerry-washington-on-not-conforming-in-hollywood.html.

10. Meadhbh McGrath, "'I Spent the First 20 Years of My Life Trying to Be Somebody Else': Kerry Washington Talks Hollywood Beauty Standards and Photoshop Fails," *Independent*, April 12, 2016, http://www.independent.ie/style /celebrity/celebrity-news/i-spent-the-first-20-years-of-my-life-trying-to-be-somebody-else-kerry-washington-talks-hollywood-beauty-standards-and-photoshop-fails-34620795 .html.

Chapter 2

1. Denzel Washington and Daniel Paisner, *A Hand to Guide Me: Legends and Leaders Celebrate the People Who Shaped Their Lives* (Des Moines, IA: Meredith, 2006).

2. Roger Ebert, review of *Our Song*, by Jim McKay, RogerEbert.com, July 6, 2001, http://www.rogerebert.com/ reviews/our-song-2001.

3. Judy Bachrach, "Kerry Washington: Her *Allure* Cover Shoot," *Allure*, October 19, 2014, http://www.allure.com/ gallery/kerry-washington.

4. "Kerry Washington, Kate Mara and More Drama Actresses on THR's Roundtable," YouTube, May 29, 2013, https:// www.youtube.com/watch?v=3-jnoStYQJw.

5. Nikki Schwab, "Kerry Washington Recalls Playing a Singing Frog During Her Time at GW," *Washington Examiner*, May 19, 2013, http://www.washingtonexaminer.com/kerry-washington-recalls-playing-a-singing-frog-during-her-time-at-gw/article/2530028.

Chapter 3

1. Carla Meyer, "'Lakeview Terrace' Actress Kerry Washington Flies Under the Radar," *PopMatters*, September 22, 2008,

http://www.popmatters.com/article/lakeview-terrace-actress-kerry-washington-flies-under-the-radar.

2. Ross Von Metzke, "Life Is Hot for Kerry Washington," *Advocate*, June 26, 2009, http://www.advocate.com/arts-entertainment/film/2009/06/26/life-hot-kerry-washington.

3. Clay Cane, "Life Is Hot for Kerry Washington," BET.com, September 15, 2010, http://www.bet.com/news/celebrities/2010/09/15/kerrywashingtonint.html.

4. "Q & A—Mother and Child's Kerry Washington on the Wayanses, Anthony Mackie, and How Good She Looks in an Afro," AMC, May 2010, http://www.amc.com/talk/2010/05/qa-mother-and.

5. Lauren Williams, "The Root Interview: Kerry Washington on 'Night Catches Us,'" *Root*, December 7, 2010, http://www.theroot.com/the-root-interview-kerry-washington-on-night-catches-u-1790881876.

Chapter 4

1. Edward Douglas, "Exclusive: Kerry Washington on For Colored Girls," ComingSoon.net, November 4, 2010, http://www.comingsoon.net/movies/features/71392-exclusive-kerry-washington-on-for-colored-girls.

2. Nigel Smith, "Exclusive Q & A: 'For Colored Girls' Star Kerry Washington," MTV News, November 5, 2010, http://www.mtv.com/news/2801087/kerry-washington-for-colored-girls.

3. Dove Clark, "For Colored Girls Full Cast Interview! Tyler Perry, Janet Jackson, Anika Noni Rose and More," *UrbLife*, October 26, 2010, http://urblife.com/the-fame/for-colored-girls-full-cast-interview.

4. Kam Williams, "Kerry Washington: The 'A Thousand Words' Interview," Skanner News, February 27, 2012, http://www.theskanner.com/entertainment/people/13474-celebrity-interview-kerry-washington-the-a-thousand-words-interview-2012-02-27.

5. Aitkenhead, "Kerry Washington: Notes on a Scandal."

6. Mark Peikert, "Kerry Washington on Going from Film to TV with 'Scandal,'" Backstage, December 18, 2012, https://www.backstage.com/interview/kerry-washington-on-going-from-tv-film-scandal.

7. Ibid.

8. Maggie Furlong, "'Scandal' on ABC: Cast and Creators on Real-Life Inspiration, Taking On the White House and More," *Huffington Post*, April 3, 2012, http://www.huffingtonpost.com/2012/04/03/scandal-abc-cast-interviews_n_1397394.html.

9. Nardine Saad, "'Scandal's' Olivia Pope Is No Role Model, Kerry Washington Says (but OK to Dress Like Her)," *Los Angeles Times*, August 5, 2015, http://www.latimes.com/entertainment/tv/showtracker/la-et-st-kerry-washington-olivia-pope-scandal-role-model-20150805-story.html.

10. Nicole Sperling, "'Django Unchained' Was More Than a Role for Kerry Washington," *Los Angeles Times*, December 31, 2012, http://articles.latimes.com/2012/dec/31/entertainment/la-et-kerry-washington-django-unchained-20130101.

Chapter 5

1. Von Metzke, "Life Is Hot for Kerry Washington."

2. Ibid.

3. "Kerry Washington Talks President's Committee on Arts and Humanities—Power of Women 2013," YouTube, October 5, 2013, https://www.youtube.com/watch?v=w0fT9ihDDI4.

4. Ibid

5. Wendy L. Wilson, "DNC Report: Kerry Washington on Why She's Voting Obama," *Essence*, September 7, 2012, http://www.essence.com/2012/09/07/dnc-report-kerry-washington-why-shes-voting-obama.

6. Kerry Washington, "Kerry Washington, Star of ABC's 'Scandal,' on Why She's Voting for Barack Obama," *Daily*

Beast, October 22, 2012, http://www.thedailybeast.com/
articles/2012/10/22/kerry-washington-star-of-abc-s-
scandal-on-why-she-s-voting-for-barack-obama.html.

7. Elyse Siegel, "Kerry Washington DNC Speech: Read the Democratic National Convention Remarks," *Huffington Post*, September 6, 2012, http://www.huffingtonpost.com/ 2012/09/06/kerry-washington-dnc-speech_n_1862985.html.

8. Julie Miller, "Hillary Clinton Answers Kerry Washington and Amy Poehler's Questions About Female Empowerment, *Vanity Fair*, July 22, 2014, http://www.vanityfair.com/ hollywood/2014/07/hillary-clinton-kerry-washington-amy-poehler.

9. Stephanie Webber, "Hillary Clinton Visits the Scandal Set, Kerry Washington and More Stars Freak Out," *Us Weekly*, February 23, 2016, http://www.usmagazine.com/ entertainment/news/hillary-clinton-visits-the-scandal-set-stars-freak-out-photos-w165118.

10. "Kerry Washington Dropping the Mic—Women's March LA 2017," YouTube, January 21, 2017, https://www.youtube.com/watch?v=itBbtXYest0.

11. Kirbie Johnson, "Kerry Washington Wants to Put This Ingredient in Every Beauty Product," POPSUGAR, March 19, 2017, https://www.popsugar.com/beauty/Kerry-Washington-Neutrogena-Interview-43219801.

12. "How Kerry Washington Is Taking a Stylish Stand Against Domestic Violence," *People*, October 30, 2014, http://people.com/celebrity/how-kerry-washington-is-taking-a-stylish-stand-against-domestic-violence.

13. Angelica Pronto, "#WomenThatDo: Kerry Washington," *Entity*, October 28, 2016, https://www.entitymag.com/ womenthatdo-kerry-washington.

14. Taylor Bryant, "Kerry Washington Surprises Fan and Sends an Important Message," *Refinery29*, April 8, 2016, http://www.refinery29.com/2016/02/103069/kerry-washington-neutrogena-makeup-interview.

15. Kristina Rodulfo, "Kerry Washington Wants to Help You Find the Right Foundation," *Elle*, February 11, 2016, http://

www.elle.com/beauty/makeup-skin-care/news/a33992/
kerry-washington-neutrogena-expand-shades.

Chapter 6

1. Shani Harris, "Kerry Washington 'Night Catches Us' Interview," YouTube, November 14, 2010, https://www.youtube.com/watch?v=vxnR7WbjSZ8.

2. Aaron Couch, "NAACP Image Awards: Winners Announced," *Hollywood Reporter*, February 1, 2013, http://www.hollywoodreporter.com/news/naacp-image-awards-winners-announced-417553.

3. "Kerry Washington 'Night Catches Us' Interview," YouTube, December 1, 2010, https://www.youtube.com/watch?v=3GR_S6n12Kc.

4. Mariah Yamamoto, "Kerry Washington Accepts the Vanguard Award at the #glaadawards," GLAAD, March 21, 2015, http://www.glaad.org/blog/video-kerry-washington-accepts-vanguard-award-glaadawards.

5. Jessica Pressler, "Kerry Washington Wants You to Ask Yourself If You're Still Blaming the Victim," *Elle*, April 11, 2016, http://www.elle.com/fashion/a34622/kerry-washington-april-2016.

6. Ibid.

7. Nellie Andreeva, "Kerry Washington Inks Overall Deal with ABC Studios," *Deadline*, April 26, 2016, http://deadline.com/2016/04/kerry-washington-overall-deal-abc-studios-1201744236.

8. Rachel Simon, "Kerry Washington Is Done Being the Only Woman in the Room," *Bustle*, January 24, 2017, https://www.bustle.com/p/kerry-washington-is-done-being-the-only-woman-in-the-room-32455.

9. Ibid.

10. Ibid.

11. "Kerry Washington Sets Up 2nd Project Under New ABC Deal—A Comedy Titled 'Melting Potts,'" *Shadow and Act*,

November 3, 2016, http://shadowandact.com/2016/11/03/kerry-washington-sets-up-2nd-project-under-new-abc-deal-a-comedy-titled-melting-potts.

12. Jodi Guglielmi, "Kerry Washington is a 'Super-Smarty-Pants' Red Sports Car in *Cars 3* First Look," *People*, March 9, 2017, http://people.com/movies/kerry-washington-cars-3-first-look.

13. Jennifer Merritt, "Kerry Washington Explains Why She Took a Social Media Hiatus Inside the New *InStyle*," *InStyle*, August 3, 2016, http://www.instyle.com/news/kerry-washington-explains-social-media-hiatus.

14. Abby Feiner, "Kerry Washington Reveals How She Hid Her Baby Bump on 'Scandal,'" *Us Weekly*, January 25, 2017, http://www.usmagazine.com/celebrity-news/news/kerry-washington-talks-hiding-her-baby-bump-on-scandal-w463043.

15. Bruna Nessif, "Kerry Washington's First Post-Baby Interview: *Scandal* Star Feels "Really Blessed" to Be a Mom," E! News, June 10, 2014, http://www.eonline.com/news/549986/kerry-washington-s-first-post-baby-interview-scandal-star-feels-really-blessed-to-be-a-mom.

16. Guglielmi, "Kerry Washington is a 'Super-Smarty-Pants' Red Sports Car."

17. Julie Naughton, "Kerry Washington Talks Scandal and OPI Nail Collection," *WWD*, January 27, 2016, http://wwd.com/beauty-industry-news/beauty-features/kerry-washington-scandal-opi-nail-collection-10329469.

GLOSSARY

accolade Award or recognition of merit.

adaptation A movie, television, or theatrical performance that has been converted from a preexisting piece of writing.

advocate Someone who publicly supports a person, cause, or policy.

anecdote A short and interesting story about a real incident and person.

anthropology The study of past and present human societies and cultures.

avenge To inflict harm on behalf of someone else; to seek revenge or punishment.

charisma Compelling attractiveness or charm that inspires other people.

choreograph To compose a sequence of steps and movement, usually to music.

chronicle To record in detail.

constraint Limitation or restriction.

entanglement A complicated or compromising relationship or situation.

guru Spiritual teacher.

homage Respect shown publicly.

iconic Widely known and acknowledged for distinctive excellence.

landmark An event that marks an important stage or turning point.

niche A comfortable or suitable position in life.

omniscient All-knowing.

protagonist The main character of a story; a leading actor or participant in a literary work or real event.

psychology The scientific study of the human mind and behavior.

recur To occur again periodically.

reprise To repeat a performance.

sociology Study of development, organization, and function of human society.

stigma Disgrace related to a specific circumstance, attribute, or person; a set of negative and usually unfair beliefs that a society or group of people hold about something.

visceral Instinctive, raw, or provoking a physical response; relating to deep inward feelings rather than the intellect.

vulnerability Openness to moral attack, criticism, or temptation; capability of being wounded.

FURTHER INFORMATION

Books

Bennett, Brit. *The Mothers*. New York: Riverhead, 2016.

Rhimes, Shonda. *Year of Yes*. New York: Simon and Schuster, 2015.

Washington, Denzel, and Daniel Paisner. *A Hand to Guide Me: Legends and Leaders Celebrate the People Who Shaped Their Lives*. Des Moines, IA.: Meredith, 2006.

Websites

Allstate Foundation Purple Purse
http://purplepurse.com

Kerry Washington advocates for victims of domestic violence through fashion as an Allstate Foundation Purple Purse ambassador. Learn about domestic violence and what Allstate is doing to help survivors find financial independence.

Internet Movie Database
http://www.imdb.com/name/nm0913488

This website allows users to learn about Kerry Washington's career, check out specific Washington films and TV shows, and even read reviews of her work.

Kerry Washington (@kerrywashington) Twitter
https://twitter.com/kerrywashington

Get information on Washington's most current projects, see her interact with fans, and share information on a variety of social movements on the actress's official Twitter page.

President's Committee on the Arts and the Humanities
https://www.pcah.gov

Kerry Washington had the distinction of serving as a member of the President's Committee on the Arts and the Humanities during the Obama administration. Find out more about current members of the committee as well as resources and programs that the committee supports.

**V-Day: A Global Movement to End Violence
Against Women and Girls**
http://www.vday.org

Kerry Washington's first V-Day performance was in 2002. She currently serves as a board member for this vital feminist organization.

Video

**George Washington University Commencement 2013:
Kerry Washington**
https://www.youtube.com/watch?v=Hl08kKKS1lw

Watch Kerry Washington tell new graduates about the importance of facing fears on the way to success in her address to George Washington University's class of 2013.

BIBLIOGRAPHY

Aitkenhead, Decca. "Kerry Washington: Notes on a Scandal." *Guardian*, June 28, 2013. https://www.theguardian.com/culture/2013/jun/28/kerry-washington-scandal-interview.

Andreeva, Nellie. "Kerry Washington Inks Overall Deal with ABC Studios." *Deadline*, April 26, 2016. http://deadline.com/2016/04/kerry-washington-overall-deal-abc-studios-1201744236.

Bachrach, Judy. "Kerry Washington: Her *Allure* Cover Shoot." *Allure*, October 19, 2014. http://www.allure.com/gallery/kerry-washington.

Bryant, Taylor. "Kerry Washington Surprises Fan and Sends an Important Message." *Refinery29*, April 8, 2016. http://www.refinery29.com/2016/02/103069/kerry-washington-neutrogena-makeup-interview.

Cane, Clay. "Life Is Hot for Kerry Washington." BET.com, September 15, 2010. http://www.bet.com/news/celebrities/2010/09/15/kerrywashingtonint.html.

Clark, Dove. "For Colored Girls Full Cast Interview! Tyler Perry, Janet Jackson, Anika Noni Rose and More!" *UrbLife*, October 26, 2010. http://urblife.com/the-fame/for-colored-girls-full-cast-interview.

Couch, Aaron. "NAACP Image Awards: Winners Announced." *Hollywood Reporter*, February 1, 2013. http://www.hollywoodreporter.com/news/naacp-image-awards-winners-announced-417553.

Douglas, Edward. "Exclusive: Kerry Washington on For Colored Girls." ComingSoon.net, November 4, 2010. http://www.

comingsoon.net/movies/features/71392-exclusive-kerry-washington-on-for-colored-girls.

Ebert, Roger. Review of *Our Song*, by Jim McKay. RogerEbert.com, July 6, 2001. http://www.rogerebert.com/reviews/our-song-2001.

Feiner, Abby. "Kerry Washington Reveals How She Hid Her Baby Bump on 'Scandal.'" *Us Weekly*, January 25, 2017. http://www.usmagazine.com/celebrity-news/news/kerry-washington-talks-hiding-her-baby-bump-on-scandal-w463043.

Furlong, Maggie. "'Scandal' on ABC: Cast and Creators on Real-Life Inspiration, Taking On the White House and More." *Huffington Post*, April 3, 2012. http://www.huffingtonpost.com/2012/04/03/scandal-abc-cast-interviews_n_1397394.html.

Guglielmi, Jodi. "Kerry Washington Is a 'Super-Smarty-Pants' Red Sports Car in *Cars 3* First Look." *People*, March 9, 2017. http://people.com/movies/kerry-washington-cars-3-first-look.

Huver, Scott. "Kerry Washington Talks 'Scandal': Olivia Pope Should Be 'Nobody's Role Model.'" AOL Moviefone, September 23, 2015. https://www.moviefone.com/2015/09/23/kerry-washington-scandal-season-4-interview.

Johnson, Kirbie. "Kerry Washington Wants to Put This Ingredient in Every Beauty Product." POPSUGAR, March 19, 2017. https://www.popsugar.com/beauty/Kerry-Washington-Neutrogena-Interview-43219801.

Kamp, David, and Jessica Diehl. "Ms. Kerry Goes to Washington: The First Lady of Scandal Speaks." *Vanity Fair*, August 2013. http://www.vanityfair.com/style/2013/08/kerry-washington-scandal-cover-story.

Kiefer, Elizabeth. "Kerry Washington Talks Race, Sexual Harassment and Her New HBO Film, *Confirmation*." *Refinery29*, April 13, 2016. http://www.refinery29.com/2016/04/107679/kerry-washington-confirmation-interview.

McGrath, Meadhbh. "'I Spent the First 20 Years of My Life Trying to Be Somebody Else': Kerry Washington Talks Hollywood Beauty Standards and Photoshop Fails." *Independent*, April 12, 2016. http://www.independent.ie/style/celebrity/celebrity-news/i-spent-the-first-20-years-of-my-life-trying-to-be-somebody-else-kerry-washington-talks-hollywood-beauty-standards-and-photoshop-fails-34620795.html.

Merritt, Jennifer. "Kerry Washington Explains Why She Took a Social Media Hiatus Inside the New *InStyle*." *InStyle*, August 3, 2016. http://www.instyle.com/news/kerry-washington-explains-social-media-hiatus.

Miller, Julie. "Hillary Clinton Answers Kerry Washington and Amy Poehler's Questions About Female Empowerment." *Vanity Fair*, July 22, 2014. http://www.vanityfair.com/hollywood/2014/07/hillary-clinton-kerry-washington-amy-poehler.

Naughton, Julie. "Kerry Washington Talks Scandal and OPI Nail Collection." *WWD*, January 27, 2016. http://wwd.com/beauty-industry-news/beauty-features/kerry-washington-scandal-opi-nail-collection-10329469.

Nessif, Bruna. "Kerry Washington's First Post-Baby Interview: *Scandal* Star Feels "Really Blessed" to Be a Mom." E! News, June 10, 2014. http://www.eonline.com/news/549986/kerry-washington-s-first-post-baby-interview-scandal-star-feels-really-blessed-to-be-a-mom.

Peikert, Mark. "Kerry Washington on Going from Film to TV with 'Scandal.'" Backstage, December 18, 2012. https://www.backstage.com/interview/kerry-washington-on-going-from-tv-film-scandal.

Peoples, Lindsay. "Kerry Washington Explains Why She Refuses to Conform to Hollywood's Beauty Standards." *New York Magazine*, April 11, 2016. http://nymag.com/thecut/2016/04/kerry-washington-on-not-conforming-in-hollywood.html.

Pressler, Jessica. "Kerry Washington Wants You to Ask Yourself If You're Still Blaming the Victim." *Elle*, April 11, 2016. http://www.elle.com/fashion/a34622/kerry-washington-april-2016.

Rhimes, Shonda. *Year of Yes*. New York: Simon and Schuster, 2015.

Rodulfo, Kristina. "Kerry Washington Wants to Help You Find the Right Foundation." *Elle*, February 11, 2016. http://www.elle.com/beauty/makeup-skin-care/news/a33992/kerry-washington-neutrogena-expand-shades.

Saad, Nardine. "'Scandal's' Olivia Pope Is No Role Model, Kerry Washington Says (but OK to Dress Like Her)." *Los Angeles Times*, August 5, 2015. http://www.latimes.com/entertainment/tv/showtracker/la-et-st-kerry-washington-olivia-pope-scandal-role-model-20150805-story.html.

Schwab, Nikki. "Kerry Washington Recalls Playing a Singing Frog During Her Time at GW." *Washington Examiner*, May 19, 2013. http://www.washingtonexaminer.com/kerry-washington-recalls-playing-a-singing-frog-during-her-time-at-gw/article/2530028.

Siegel, Elyse. "Kerry Washington DNC Speech: Read the Democratic National Convention Remarks." *Huffington Post*, September 6, 2012. http://www.huffingtonpost.com/2012/09/06/kerry-washington-dnc-speech_n_1862985.html.

Simon, Rachel. "Kerry Washington Is Done Being the Only Woman in the Room." *Bustle*, January 24, 2017. https://www.bustle.com/p/kerry-washington-is-done-being-the-only-woman-in-the-room-32455.

Smith, Nigel. "Exclusive Q & A: 'For Colored Girls' Star Kerry Washington." MTV News, November 5, 2010. http://www.mtv.com/news/2801087/kerry-washington-for-colored-girls.

Sperling, Nicole. "'Django Unchained' Was More Than a Role for Kerry Washington." *Los Angeles Times*, December 31, 2012. http://articles.latimes.com/2012/dec/31/entertainment/la-et-kerry-washington-django-unchained-20130101.

Von Metzke, Ross. "Life Is Hot for Kerry Washington." *Advocate*, June 26, 2009. http://www.advocate.com/arts-entertainment/film/2009/06/26/life-hot-kerry-washington.

Washington, Kerry. "Kerry Washington, Star of ABC's 'Scandal,' on Why She's Voting for Barack Obama." *Daily Beast*, October 22, 2012. http://www.thedailybeast.com/articles/2012/10/22/kerry-washington-star-of-abc-s-scandal-on-why-she-s-voting-for-barack-obama.html.

Webber, Stephanie. "Hillary Clinton Visits the Scandal Set, Kerry Washington and More Stars Freak Out." *Us Weekly*, February 23, 2016. http://www.usmagazine.com/entertainment/news/hillary-clinton-visits-the-scandal-set-stars-freak-out-photos-w165118.

Wieselman, Jarett. "Kerry Washington's Journey from Girl to Gladiator." BuzzFeed, January 31, 2014. https://www.buzzfeed.com/jarettwieselman/kerry-washingtons-journey-from-girl-to-gladiator?utm_term=.kfaa9wa3Q#.pe4wKewP3.

Williams, Kam. "Kerry Washington: The 'A Thousand Words' Interview." Skanner News, February 27, 2012. http://www.theskanner.com/entertainment/people/13474-celebrity-interview-kerry-washington-the-a-thousand-words-interview-2012-02-27.

Williams, Lauren. "The Root Interview: Kerry Washington on 'Night Catches Us.'" *Root*, December 7, 2010. http://www.theroot.com/the-root-interview-kerry-washington-on-night-catches-u-1790881876.

Wilson, Wendy L. "DNC Report: Kerry Washington on Why She's Voting Obama." *Essence*, September 7, 2012. http://www.essence.com/2012/09/07/dnc-report-kerry-washington-why-shes-voting-obama.

INDEX

ABOUT THE AUTHOR

Joel Newsome is a writer and movie buff living in Massachusetts. He has written several other books about a variety of subjects from the history of the mythology of elves to the great military strategist Hannibal Barca.